Building Blocks

A play

Bob Larbey

Samuel French — London
New York - Toronto - Hollywood

Copyright © 1994 by Bob Larbey
All Rights Reserved

BUILDING BLOCKS is fully protected under the copyright laws of the British Commonwealth, including Canada, the United States of America, and all other countries of the Copyright Union. All rights, including professional and amateur stage productions, recitation, lecturing, public reading, motion picture, radio broadcasting, television and the rights of translation into foreign languages are strictly reserved.

ISBN 978-0-573-11086-3

www.samuelfrench.co.uk
www.samuelfrench.com

For Amateur Production Enquiries

United Kingdom and World excluding North America

plays@SamuelFrench-London.co.uk

020 7255 4302/01

Each title is subject to availability from Samuel French, depending upon country of performance.

CAUTION: Professional and amateur producers are hereby warned that BUILDING BLOCKS is subject to a licensing fee. Publication of this play does not imply availability for performance. Both amateurs and professionals considering a production are strongly advised to apply to the appropriate agent before starting rehearsals, advertising, or booking a theatre. A licensing fee must be paid whether the title is presented for charity or gain and whether or not admission is charged.

The professional rights in this play are controlled by The Agency (London) Ltd, 24 Pottery Lane, Holland Park, London W11 4LZ.

No one shall make any changes in this title for the purpose of production. No part of this book may be reproduced, stored in a retrieval system, or transmitted in any form, by any means, now known or yet to be invented, including mechanical, electronic, photocopying, recording, videotaping, or otherwise, without the prior written permission of the publisher. No one shall upload this title, or part of this title, to any social media websites.

The right of Bob Larbey to be identified as author of this work has been asserted in accordance with Section 77 of the Copyright, Designs and Patents Act 1988.

BUILDING BLOCKS

First performed, in an earlier version, at the Nuffield Theatre, Southampton, on 22nd September 1992, with the following cast:

Mark	Steve Edwin
Piper	Stephen Bent
Jim Baxter	Philip Bretherton
Mary Baxter	Kate Spiro
David	Christopher Timothy
Dave	Mark Letheren
Brian	John Forgeham

Director Patrick Sandford
Set and Costume Designer Robin Don
Costume Designer Nicole Young
Lighting Designer Stephen Watson
Deputy Stage Manager Nicola Wingfield

The action takes place in the garden of the Baxters' house in the not too rural countryside

ACT I

SCENE 1	A summer afternoon
SCENE 2	Morning. The following Wednesday

ACT II

SCENE 1	A month later
SCENE 2	The following day
SCENE 3	The following day
SCENE 4	Three months later

CHARACTERS

Mark, a bricklayer
Piper, a bricklayer
Jim Baxter
Mary Baxter
David, the builder
Brian, a carpenter

ACT I

Scene 1

The back of the Baxters' house. Afternoon. Summer

An extension is being built on to the R of the existing house, at a right angle to it; the brickwork shell of the extension is complete and is surrounded by scaffolding and ladders. The back door of the house (over which is a porch) leads on to a patio, on which is a garden seat; the lawn in front of the patio has two garden chairs, a bench and a mess of scaffolding, timber and bricks on it, as well as a hand-built truss which takes up a great deal of room. Leading off L is an incomplete path with spare paving slabs stacked nearby; also L is a cement mixer

There are four entrances into the garden: from the front of the house, round the extension (R), from the back garden and woods (L) through the back door of the house and from the first floor of the extension via the scaffolding and ladders. A window next to the door allows a view of a portion of the kitchen beyond

When the CURTAIN *rises, Mark and Piper, two young bricklayers, are sitting in the garden having their tea break. They both have sandwiches; the mugs of tea on a tray are obviously courtesy of the Baxters*

Mark That was quite a nice lawn when we started.
Piper (*not overly interested*) Mm.
Mark They'll have it re-turfed, I expect. Quicker than seeding. Nearly always comes up patchy, seeding.
Piper A bit like your hair.
Mark (*bothered*) I'm not bothered. I'm not vain.
Piper Just as well really.
Mark How's your rash by the way? Do you think you'll have that all your life?
Piper It's an allergy.
Mark That's really only another way of saying a nervous disorder.

Piper attacks Mark in what is obviously a familiar pattern of mock fighting

Jim Baxter comes on L. He is about thirty-five and carries a briefcase

Piper and Mark spring apart

Jim Hallo lads.
Mark Hallo Mr Baxter.
Piper Mr Baxter.
Jim Home early today. Mrs Wilson has my little lot for Art, so I thought I'd slip away — artfully. (*He laughs at his own little joke*)

Mark and Piper manage weak smiles

Jim looks at the extension; it is quite obvious that he has no professional knowledge of building

My word, this is all going very well, isn't it? I notice the difference every day I come home from school, you know.

Mark and Piper smile politely

How's the cricket going then, Mark? Did you play Saturday?
Mark Oh. Yes.
Piper He was out second ball.
Jim Oh dear. Brian's not back yet then?
Mark He's got to finish up at The Manor you see.
Piper Tuesday.
Jim Well, that's not so bad, is it? Obviously a big job up at The Manor. Big roof, I suppose. Tuesday's not so bad. Not so bad at all.

Jim exits through the back door of the house

Piper He'll be out again in a minute. "Mark," he'll say, "could I have a word?"
Mark He should talk to David, not me.
Piper He has to find David first.
Mark Yes. What is it that tells him to hop into his Range Rover and disappear into the wide blue yonder just before the phone rings in his office?
Piper Animal instinct, I reckon.
Mark You'd think he'd have a phone in the Range Rover.

Act I Scene 1   3

Piper Would you?
Mark } (*together*) No.
Piper
Piper Hey-up, here he comes.

Jim enters from the house

Jim Mark, could I have a word?
Mark Yes, Mr Baxter?
Jim This Brian business. I hadn't realized it had been two weeks.
Mark Is it as long as that?
Jim Yes it is, and, as Mary points out, he did come to start here and, well, we did imagine that once here he'd stay until the job was finished.
Mark Well, he would under normal circumstances.
Jim Now look, Mark, if circumstances are anything other than normal, it's hardly our fault, is it?
Piper Tuesday has been mentioned.
Jim I know it's been mentioned, Piper, but quite honestly, Mary is ... well, she's getting a bit cynical about it all.
Mark Look, I'll pop into the office on my way home tonight and leave a note for David.
Jim I'd be very grateful. You won't forget?
Mark No, no.

Jim exits into the house

Piper The only way you'll get David to read a note is to nail it to his forehead.

There is the sound of a lorry in low gear off R. *The horn sounds*

Piper It's Slater's with the timber. (*Calling* R) Hallo Ernie!
Mark (*looking off* R) He's too close to that gatepost! (*He calls* R) Ernie! You're too close to the gatepost!
Piper (*calling* R) Ernie!

Mark and Piper run off R *but it is too late. There is a thump and the sound of the rending of wood*

Mary enters from the house, followed by Jim

Mary Now look what they've done! They're paying for that! David's paying for that!
Jim Of course he will. There's no question of that.
Mary I want a new gatepost!
Jim Absolutely. We'll insist on it.
Mary Did you ask Mark about the carpenter?
Jim Oh yes. He's going to leave David a note.
Mary What's the use of that? I'm sure the first thing he does every morning is burn all the notes on his desk. Ring him up.
Jim I've only just got home.
Mary And I've been here all day — every day for five months! You don't know what it's like.
Jim I know it hasn't been easy, love. But think of the end result.
Mary What end result? There's never going to be an end result. We're going to live with the shell of an extension and half a roof for the rest of our lives! Please phone David. Please phone David!
Jim All right, love, all right.

He exits into the house

Mark enters from the R

Mark I'm sorry about the gatepost.
Mary It wasn't your fault, Mark.
Mark We'll stack the timber up the front, shall we?
Mary If you like. Only you'll mind the roses won't you?
Mark Oh absolutely.
Mary What timber?
Mark For the rest of the trusses.
Mary Oh yes. The carpenter makes those, doesn't he? (*A short laugh*) The carpenter!
Mark Look, once he's here ...
Mary Oh yes. Once he's here. Are all extensions like this?
Mark More or less. You'll forget about all the problems when it's finished.
Mary Everyone says that.

Jim enters from the house, looking pleased with himself

Jim I got David. He'll be round in five minutes; there you are.
Mary Good God!

Act I Scene 1

Mark We'll get on with off-loading the timber then.
Jim Are you stacking it down here? Probably the best place.
Mark No. Up the front.
Jim Oh fine. Good. You'll mind the roses?
Mark Absolutely.

He exits R, saying the following as he goes

Mind the roses, Ernie!
Jim (*pleased with himself*) You see, at the end of the day, things aren't going too badly, are they?
Mary No. (*She starts, as if realizing what she she has said*) Jim, he hasn't been yet!
Jim Who hasn't?
Mary David, the builder I made you phone against your will.
Jim We don't make each other do things, love.
Mary (*picking up the tray of tea-things and heading for the house*) All right, we'll forget that bit. But the fact is the telephone call was made to complain. And what are you doing? You're saying, "Things aren't going too badly" before he even gets here!

She exits into the house

Jim Look, we talked about this before we started the extension. Nerves are bound to jangle a bit.

Mary enters from the house without the tray

Mary Yes, mine, but you don't seem to care.
Jim Of course I care, but there's no point being up in the air all the time, is there? Anyway, we break up on Monday. I'll be home for the holidays. Then I can pull things together — take the weight off your shoulders. I know it hasn't been easy for you.
Mary No, it hasn't.
Jim But from Monday I'll be at home. I'll get on top of things.
Mary Will you really?
Jim Promise. It's going to be beautiful when it's finished, you know.
Mary Yes.

There is the sound of a car pulling up

Mary There's David.
Jim In less than five minutes.
Mary You will be firm with him, won't you?
Jim Yes, but I'll be firm with him in my own way. I don't think you get anywhere by shouting.
Mary I'm not asking you to shout.
Jim No, I know, so I won't. Agreed?
Mary You do the talking.

They arrange themselves defensively

David, the builder, enters R. He is big, bluff and does have a way with him

David Hallo Mary. Hallo Jim. Lovely day isn't it? Five minutes I said. The new timbers have come, I see. Very reliable people, Slaters.
Mary They knocked the gatepost down.
David Did they? Did they? I thought it was at an angle.
Jim We'll want that replaced, David.
David Of course you will. (*He takes out a notebook and pen*) Of course you will. My goodness, of course you will. (*He writes*) "One gatepost, straightened up and made good."
Mary There's a chunk out of it.
David (*writing*) "And chamfer damaged edge."
Jim Chamfer?
David Jim, you won't know the difference, I promise. It'll give it a bit of character. I always think that gateposts profit from a bit of chamfering. I'm surprised the people here before you didn't have it chamfered in the first place.

Jim nods in agreement, but Mary nudges him

Jim Nevertheless David, they didn't. And, also nevertheless, the fact is that the gatepost has been damaged by one of your lorries.
David Now that's not strictly true. One of Slaters' lorries. But — and I say this in all good faith — it is down to me to make good the damage.
Jim Thank you.
David We can set it straight, of course we can, but if you really insist on a new gatepost altogether ——
Mary We want a new gatepost!
David Then a new gatepost you shall have. Of course, we'll need to drill down; that's well-bedded, that post. We're going to have to rip up at least

Act I Scene 1

two feet down the drive — say three across. Then you'll need new hard-core ——

Mary Just straighten it.

Jim Probably best.

David Wise choice. And it's not a penny on the bill, don't you worry about that. Now is there anything else?

Jim No, I don't think so.

Mary Brian! There's Brian! David, we had a carpenter for three days and then he disappeared. We want him back!

David That's why I use Brian, you know. He's a craftsman. I never buy in ready-made trusses, you know. Brian makes them all by hand. Something to boast about, that will be. You'll be able to take people up to your loft and say, "Look at that! Those trusses were hand-built for our house. Not anybody's house. Our house!"

Mary But we don't have enough.

David Enough what?

Mary Enough trusses! We don't have a carpenter, so he hasn't made them all, let alone put them up!

Jim Now that is true, David.

David Ah.

Mary The Manor?

Jim Yes. Now I realize, David, that The Manor is probably — well, certainly — a bigger job than ours. It may make our extension look like a piddling little job, but the way we see it ——

David How long have I known you, Jim?

Jim I don't know. Since we moved down. Five or six years.

David And we live in the same village, don't we?

Jim Well, yes.

David And do you seriously think that I would describe your extension as a "piddling little job"?

Jim No, they were my words.

David Certainly not mine.

Mary Then why is The Manor getting preferential treatment all the time?

David Mary, it isn't. I'm sorry to say this, because I don't like criticizing my own staff, but the fault lies with Charlie in the office.

Mary Why?

David He should never have sent Brian round here for those three days in the first place. If Brian hadn't come for those three days, you wouldn't have been upset about him going back to The Manor because you wouldn't have seen him to begin with.

Mary and Jim look as if they are trying to take this in

I was off with flu, you see. I mean, Charlie's very good in his own way but — and I have to say this — he's too eager to please. I like the man enormously but he will not think things through. I'm going to have to take him to task over this. (*He takes out his notebook and pen again*) Note to self: "Take Charlie to task."
Jim No, don't do that.
Mary I'm sure he acted for the best.
Jim We're not angry with him.
David You've every right to be.
Jim No, don't mention it to him. I'm sure it was an honest mistake.
David Oh it wouldn't be anything else but honest. I expect he's still worried about his little girl's hearing.
Mary His little girl?
David She's got to see a specialist in London next week.
Mary Oh dear. What's wrong with her?
David They don't know, you see. That's why she's seeing a specialist — next Tuesday. I'll probably drive them up myself, Charlie obviously being concerned — well, you don't want him on the M25 in that frame of mind, do you?
Jim Absolutely not.
David Those of us blessed with good health should be very grateful, shouldn't we?
Mary How old is his little girl?
David Only four.
Mary Oh.
David Still, "Ours is not to reason why" and so forth. Well, I'll be off then. I'm going shooting on Sunday. I'll drop you round a brace of pheasants. Bye now!
Mary Goodbye David.
Jim Thanks for coming.
David Not at all. Bye!

He exits R

Mary Four years old.
Jim So young.
Mary If we get lucky ——
Jim And we will.
Mary — and we will ... It's riskier with older parents.

Act I Scene 1

Jim (*putting his arm round Mary*) Oh, come on, love. All kids have little ailments of some sort.
Mary But a specialist ...
Jim Yes I know. She'll be all right.
Mary Yes.
Jim Nice of David to take them up to London himself.
Mary Yes. We will be lucky, won't we?
Jim Of course we will.
Mary And we'll keep trying.
Jim Don't make it sound like a chore.
Mary I didn't mean to make it sound like that.
Jim Anyway, we'd look silly with a bigger house and nobody to share it with us. Look, I'll tell you what. Let's go out to dinner tonight. Nice food, red wine. You know how red wine makes me feel.
Mary Not too much.
Jim No, I know what you mean. Just enough. You'll wear the black ... ?
Mary Oh yes.
Jim Good-oh. And we won't talk about the extension over dinner because, let's be honest, we knew there would be snags—inevitably. But we've had a very straight talk with David and I think we all know where we stand now.
Mary It just gets lonely trying to deal with everything on your own. It gets you down.
Jim Of course it does.
Mary You'd best book a table.
Jim Right. Yes.
Mary Try to get the one by the window. (*She heads towards the house*)
Jim If it's not already booked, yes.
Mary You will ask for it?

Mary exits into the house

Jim goes to follow Mary into the house. As he does so:

Mark enters R from the front gate

Mark I'm ever so sorry, Mr Baxter. We've squashed some of your roses.
Jim (*not wanting to break Mary's mood*) Not now Mark. Not now!

Jim exits

CURTAIN

Scene 2

The same. The following Wednesday. Morning

There is now a pile of cement by the mixer

Mark and Piper are sitting in the garden having their tea-break

Mark is combing his hair. He looks at his comb with suspicion

Piper Your pillow must look like a barber's shop floor in the morning.
Mark I'd rather lose a bit of hair than have a nervous disorder.
Piper It's an allergy.
Mark Allergy then. The trouble with allergies is, it can take years to find out what you're allergic to — decades even.
Piper You'll be as bald as a billiard-ball by then.

Jim enters from the back door

Jim Morning, lads. Everything all right?
Mark Yes thank you, Mr Baxter.
Piper Yes thank you, Mr Baxter.
Jim Good, good. (*He looks anxiously off* R. *He wants the carpenter desperately. To Mark and Piper*) I'm not standing over you or anything. School holidays. I've broken up now.
Piper Nice.

Jim looks off R *again*

Mark Sorry about the roses on Friday. It was Ernie. He will not look where he's treading.
Jim It was only two bushes. Any sign of ... ?
Mark Brian? No. He's probably finishing up at The Manor — getting his tools together.
Piper Something like that.
Jim I suppose we're getting a bit jittery. Well, Mary is getting a bit jittery.

Mark and Piper look nervous, as if they know the danger signs

Mark⎫
Piper⎭ (*together*) Well ...

Act I Scene 2

They stand up

Jim Did you play cricket on Saturday, Mark?
Mark Yes.
Jim How did you get on?
Mark I was run out.
Piper For two.
Jim Oh dear. Bad luck, that.

There is the sound of a car approaching R. They all look off R. The car continues past

Mark Well ...
Piper Well ...
Jim Back up the old scaffold?
Mark No, there's not a lot more we can do to the brickwork at the moment. You see, until we're battened and felted in, there's not really anything else we can do.
Jim Who does the battens?
Mark Oh, we can do them.
Jim Can't you start?
Mark Not until the trusses are in.
Piper And Brian does the trusses.
Jim Yes, I thought he might.
Mark But we'll carry on with the path. It's looking very nice. Have you seen it?

Jim goes to the incomplete path and treads along it

Mark and Piper take the opportunity to slip away R

Jim Yes, it's looking very nice. Very nice. In fact ... (*He sees that Mark and Piper have gone*) Oh. (*He looks hopefully off R for signs of Brian. There are none, so he calls into the house*) Mary! I think I'll stroll down to the village and get some odds and ends! (*He starts to move away R*)

Before he can exit Mary enters quickly from the house

Mary He's not here again, is he?
Jim Brian?

Mary Yes, of course Brian! Where is he?
Jim I'm not a conjuror, love.
Mary What odds and ends?
Jim Pardon?
Mary "I think I'll stroll down to the village and get some odds and ends."
Jim Yes, you know. Bits and pieces.
Mary Is that as well as or instead of?
Jim I thought it would save you going out.
Mary No you didn't. You thought it would get you out of the way. No questions to answer. Bury your head in the sand getting odds and ends and bits and pieces and hope that somehow, magically, everything will be all right by the time you get back!
Jim Mark thinks he may be packing up.
Mary (*alarmed*) Mark? Why? Where's he going?
Jim No, not Mark. Brian. Mark thinks that Brian might be packing up at The Manor before coming over here.
Mary And what do you think?
Jim I'll tell you what I think. I think we had a lovely weekend. No noise, no hassle — and I think that not once did we think about when Brian would turn up.
Mary Oh Jim, we didn't *talk* about it. It was like an unspoken pact. We didn't *talk* about it.
Jim All right, but why get so jumpy about it when it's only ten o'clock in the morning?
Mary Because he's not coming. The trusses that are up are dying of old age and we both know Brian isn't coming!
Jim You seem to forget the very frank talk we had with David on Friday. You agreed with me on Friday.
Mary Yes, I agreed with you on Friday. I wanted to agree with you on Friday. I wanted a nice evening out. I wanted to make a baby when we came home, and, most of all, I wanted to believe that, just for once, David wasn't shooting us another line.
Jim I don't think that's entirely fair. We talked things through.
Mary And what did we establish? At the end of the conversation, what did we establish? We established that the office made a mistake by ever sending us a carpenter in the first place and that Charlie's little girl has a hearing problem!
Jim You get too involved, love, that's the problem.
Mary Of course I get involved! It's my bloody house! Our house.
Jim I expect everyone feels like this when they have an extension.

Act I Scene 2

Mary No they don't. Ours is special. It's for the baby.
Jim We hope it's for the baby.
Mary No!
Jim Mary, you mustn't think of it as some sort of talisman.
Mary (*stubbornly*) It's for the baby.
Jim Look, it's a lovely day. Let's stroll down to the village. We can have a drink at the *King's Arms* and maybe by the time we get back, Brian will be here.
Mary Jim, you're living in some sort of dream world.
Jim Not necessarily. Mark said he was finishing off at The Manor.
Mary "Maybe".
Jim All right — "Maybe finishing off".
Mary And he said "clearing up", not "finishing off".
Jim Now you're just splitting hairs. It means the same thing.
Mary Yes it does. It means Brian's not here and he's not coming — ever!

Mary exits, stalking into the house

Jim That's the spirit! That's the spirit!

He exits after her

Mark and Piper come round the side of the house R

Piper They've started shouting at each other.
Mark Well I don't blame her.
Piper Feminist!
Mark No. It's always the same with extensions. The women take all the flak. They're in the firing line.
Piper Who's shooting at them?
Mark Us — all of us. Brickies, chippies, sparks. We could be robots with tape recorders in our heads. A woman asks a question, we press "Play" and out it comes — a stream of technical jargon guaranteed to make her feel like an idiot, us sound like geniuses and all designed to say Sweet Fanny Adams.
Piper Why is it the woman who's asking all these questions?
Mark Because it's usually the woman who's at home all day. What does the average husband see? Us at work when he leaves for work and us long gone by the time he comes home from work.
Piper Ah, but this one's broken up from school. He's home now.

Mark Then we'll see what he's made of then, won't we? (*He takes a packet of mints from his pocket and offers Piper one*) Mint?
Piper Ta. (*He wipes his hands*)

Mark pops a mint in Piper's mouth for him

He seems a calm sort of bloke.
Mark He's like a pressure cooker with the lid screwed down. If he blows there'll be mixed vegetables all over the ceiling of his extension.
Piper He hasn't got a ceiling to his extension.
Mark I wonder when Brian *will* come?
Piper Tuesday.
Mark It's Wednesday.
Piper So it is. Shall I cut some more slabs for the path?
Mark No. Cut some more slabs for the path.
Piper Right.

Piper exits L

Mark sorts through some of the slabs already by the path. As he does so ...

David enters R. *For once it is a quiet entrance*

The high-pitched whine of an angle-grinder starts, off L

David Mark!
Mark Hallo Boss.
David Are they in?
Mark Yes. I'll give them a shout.
David No, no. Look, the thing is we're behind with the roof-tiles at The Manor, so I want you and Piper to ——

The noise of the angle-grinder stops

Piper enters L

Piper Hallo Boss.
David Keep going! Keep going!

Piper exits L *and the noise starts again; during the following it stops again*

Mark You want me and Piper to do what?

Act I Scene 2

David Pop up to The Manor for a couple of days and help out, you know.
Mark (*nodding towards the house*) They won't like it. *She* won't like it.
David Good Heavens, it's only for a couple of days.
Mark But we're on the path.
David Look Mark, you've got a head on your shoulders. Since when has a path taken precedence over roof-tiles?
Mark Well ...
David Well there you are then. Nip off when they're not looking — best way. (*He heads for the exit* R)

As David nears the exit, Jim enters from the back door at speed, as if propelled by Mary

Jim Don't push! David!

Mary follows Jim out

David (*as though he had meant to come to see them anyway*) Ah, there you are. I was just coming to see you.
Jim Good, because ...
David I thought you'd like to hear the good news.
Jim What good news?
David (*as though there should be no other*) Little Naomi's ears.

Mark shakes his head and exits L *to re-join Piper off*

Mary Oh yes, of course. How are they? How is she?
David Wax.
Mary Wax?
David Yes. That's all it turned out to be — a build-up of wax in the ears, thank the Lord. Mind you, I don't mind telling you that waiting outside that consulting room was one of the longest fifteen minutes in my life.
Jim That's very good news though, isn't it? Very good news.
Mary Couldn't Doctor Ringwood have found out that it was only wax in her ears?
David I like John Ringwood. He'll always come out for an emergency and if it wasn't for him, the Bowls Club would have folded years ago. But I have to say this. He is specialist mad. Present him with anything that can't be classed as a viral infection and he'll have you off to a specialist before you can sit down.
Mary We wanted to phone you yesterday about Brian not turning up, but of course you weren't there.

David I was in London.

Mary All for wax in the ears.

David With respect, my dear, wisdom after the event. Would you be taking me to task if they'd found something seriously wrong? Would you have wanted Charlie driving back on the M25 knowing that he was going to have to learn sign language to communicate with his four-year-old daughter?

Mary No, of course not.

Jim No, of course not.

David No, because you're decent people.

Mary All right, David. I'm pleased for Charlie. I'm pleased for little Naomi.

David She calls me "Uncle David" you know.

Mary Does she? But it is Wednesday and we still haven't got a carpenter!

David I know, I know, and I promise you that I feel badly about it. I've let you down.

Mary Yes you have.

Jim There's something you should know, David. I've broken up for the summer holidays and I shall be making sure that you don't let us down again. Why *did* you let us down?

David No excuse at all. Not what I'd try to convince you was an excuse.

Jim Oh I see.

Mary Try us.

David You know old Ronnie Randall?

Mary No.

David Yes you do. He was here for a couple of days back in April, helping with the pillars.

Jim Oh yes. Nice chap.

David Well, something happened to him.

Mary He didn't get wax in his ears, did he?

David You did ask.

Mary Sorry.

David No, it's his cat.

Mary His cat?

David Yes — a black and white job. Ronnie's had him for years. Anyway, yesterday Ronnie had an appointment to take the cat to the vet's — routine injection, nothing more. Ronnie's missus couldn't take him you see, because of her allergy to dogs.

Jim Dogs?

Mary Possibility of dogs in the vet's waiting-room?

David You've got it. So Ronnie brought the cat up to The Manor with him, with my previous permission, to take him to the vet's for a ten o'clock

Act I Scene 2

appointment. He had him in a basket, but you know what contrary animals cats can be. Anyway, to cut a long story short, it got out.
Mary This is about why we still don't have a carpenter, isn't it?
David Of course it is. One floorboard Brian had left to put down in the hall — one floorboard! He turned to pick up the board and the cat went down that hole like a flash. Ronnie tried everything. Calling it, threatening it, telling it it was tea-time. Would it come out?
Mary No.
David No. And here's where you come in. They could see the cat, that was what was so frustrating. So Brian eases up one floorboard and what does the cat do? Backs away. Another floorboard and it backs away again. And so on and so on and do you know what? By the time they got that cat, all Brian had left was a pile of boards and the floor back to the joists.
Jim I see! Then it must have taken Brian the rest of the day to get the floorboards back down.
David Exactly!
Mary Which he did?
David He worked like a Trojan.
Mary But he got the floorboards back?
David He did, he did.
Mary So why isn't he here today?
David He'll be here tomorrow.
Mary (*getting angry*) Now just a minute!
Jim All right, love. Now just a minute, David! Why isn't he here today?
David He's sharpening his tools.
Mary Oh God. (*She puts her head in the cement-mixer and screams into it*) Oh God!
David It's only a day, Mary. He's very conscientious, Brian — always sharpens his tools for a new job. And once he's here, he'll see the job right through, and that's a promise — barring emergencies.
Jim They're not likely, are they?
David No, not *likely*.
Mary Just possible.
David Anything's possible in the building trade, Mary. You would not credit some of the things that happen.
Mary Oh I would. I would.
David (*looking at his watch*) Good Lord, is that the time? I'm supposed to be seeing Mrs Steadman about the bulge in her flank wall. There wasn't anything else was there?
Jim No, I don't think so. Mary?

Mary The gatepost.
David Right. I'll make a note of that. (*He takes out his note-book and pen*)
Mary You already did.
David Of course I did, yes. I'll get on to old man Slater about that.
Mary And his driver crushed three rose-bushes under Brian's timbers.
David Did he? Did he?
Jim Two rose-bushes actually.
David That'll be Ernie. Notoriously heavy-footed, that man is. (*He writes*) "Replace two rose-bushes." Anything else?
Jim I can't think of anything.
Mary Tiles! You were going to bring us some sample tiles for the hall.
David Was I?
Mary I phoned Charlie two weeks ago and he said you were.
David Well he didn't say anything to me. I'm not shifting the blame, but he definitely didn't. Worrying about little Naomi's ears, I suppose. What sort of tiles had you talked about?
Mary Brownish — light brownish. Charlie said something about a German firm.
David Right, you leave that with me. That's it, then? Good. Bye-bye!

David exits R

Jim Bye David.
Mary Bye David.
Jim It's stopped.
Mary What has?
Jim That noise.
Mary That was an angle-grinder.
Jim Was it?
Mary I've got used to it. It does show that something's actually happening, you see. (*She sits in a garden chair*)
Jim Cheer up, love. We get a carpenter tomorrow.
Mary Do we?
Jim Let's have some coffee. I'll make us some coffee.
Mary Yes, let's have some coffee.

David enters R *carrying a brace of pheasants*

David Nearly forgot. I said I'd bring you a brace of pheasants. (*He drops the pheasants in Mary's lap*)

Act I Scene 2

Mary Thank you.
David Mind the shot now. Lovely birds. Bye!
Mary Bye David.
Jim Bye David.

David exits R

Mary (*plainly not liking the birds in her lap*) Will you take them? Will you *take* them?

Jim gingerly picks up the pheasants

They look so sad.
Jim Well they'd hardly look happy.
Mary I've never had a bird with all its feathers and its head still on.

Jim wanders about with the birds. Mary follows him

Jim I think you're supposed to hang them. Ah! (*He spots a hook on the porch and hangs the pheasants on it*)
Mary (*looking at the pheasants swinging there*) For how long?
Jim (*looking at his watch*) I don't know.
Mary I don't think I want them.
Jim No, I don't think I do.
Mary Let's give them to Mark and Piper.
Jim (*unhooking the pheasants*) No, we can't do that. David might find out. It wouldn't look very polite, would it?

The pheasants nearly brush Mary's face.

Mary I don't want them! I don't want them!
Jim All right, all right. Look, when everybody's gone, I'll go down the garden and chuck them in the woods.
Mary Will they be all right?
Jim They *are* dead!

Mark can be heard whistling off R

Jim panics and puts the pheasants into the cement mixer, then moves quickly away

Mark enters, puts some cement in the mixer, and switches it on

Mary and Jim look on in horror

Brian, the carpenter, enters R *carrying his tool-bag and a saw-horse*

Brian Morning labourers!
Mark Good God, it's a brain surgeon!
Brian I'll be wasting my time with you, then, won't I?
Jim It's Brian!
Mary It's a carpenter!

Mary and Jim rush over to Brian as though he might be the new Messiah

Brian Morning. Do you mind if I leave my tools in your garage?
Mary You're not going already?
Brian No, I mean on a regular basis. Save me humping them home every night.
Mary You're staying!
Brian So far as I'm concerned.
Jim David said you wouldn't be here till tomorrow. He said you were sharpening your tools. Why would he say that?
Mary It's finally caught up with him. He's started making excuses before he actually has to.
Brian Well ...
Mary We were just going to have a cup of coffee. (*Warmly*) Would you like a cup of coffee, Brian?
Brian I never say no.
Mary What about Mark and Piper?
Brian Drinking from muddy puddles is more their mark.
Jim We'll all have a cup of coffee!
Mary And biscuits. I've got a new tin of biscuits!

Mary hurries off into the house

(*Calling*) Mark! Piper! We're having coffee!
Mark ⎫
Piper ⎭ (*together*) Right!

Brian starts to take his saw-horse up the ladder to put it on the scaffolding

Jim You're the key, you see. It's reached the point where you're the key.

Act I Scene 2   21

Brian It's usually like that. It's an awesome responsibility — awesome.

Jim fervently shakes Brian's hand and exits into the house

Mark and Piper enter round the corner R

Mark It's like the second coming when the chippie turns up, isn't it?
Brian Bless you my children.
Mark Your turn will come though. You'll pale into insignificance when they're waiting for a painter.
Piper Or a plumber.
Mark Or the plasterers.
Piper Or the electrician.
Mark Tinkering jobs really, all of them. Personally I think that the brickies are the unsung heroes of the building trade.
Brian Yes, you would.

Jim enters from the house with a tin of biscuits

Jim Here we are lads — biscuits. Dig in. Help yourselves. Coffee won't be long. Sit yourselves down.

Mark and Piper immediately take the two garden chairs

Jim Ah. There's another chair round the side.
Brian I'll get it.
Jim No, no. You stay there Brian. I'll get it.

Jim goes off L *to get the chair*

Piper I assume you'll want a cushion?
Brian Only if it's duck-down.
Mark They're nice people, that's the trouble.
Brian Did I denote a pang of conscience?
Mark David's mucking them about.
Brian David mucks everybody about.

Jim comes back with the chair for Brian

Jim One chair. Sit yourself down, Brian.
Brian Thank you. (*He sits*)

Jim (*looking at his three-man work-force and rubbing his hands together*)
We're on the move now! We're on the move!
Brian We're on the move now!

Jim exits into the house

Mark stares moodily into space

Brian Oh God! (*He notices Mark*) What's the matter with him?
Piper His hair's still coming out in handfuls.
Mark David wants me and Piper up at The Manor for a couple of days.
Brian The big battalions win again.

Mary enters with a tray; on it are coffee-mugs, a jug of milk and jar of Coffee-mate

Mary Coffee up! (*She sets the tray down*) Help yourselves. There's milk or Coffee-mate.
Brian
Mark } (*together*) Thank you Mrs Baxter.
Piper
Mary You will be staying?
Brian Absolutely.
Mary Oh good.
Brian So far as I'm concerned.
Mary I mean, we do *deserve* you now, don't we?

Mary exits into the house

Brian takes a tenon saw from his bag, then a loaf of bread. He cuts off a slice, replaces the bread in the bag and then takes out a tub of butter. He spreads butter on the bread with a chisel and completes the sandwich by adding a slice of ham from his pocket

Piper Fancy deserving you.
Mark Slip off after the break, that's what David said.
Brian Leaving me to explain, I suppose?
Mark I don't think he knows you're here.
Brian Where does he think I am then?

Act I Scene 2

Mark You *will* explain?
Brian Oh no. I'm not getting into all that. That's for David to do. I shall just say I turned my back for two minutes and you disappeared.
Mark Oh thanks a bundle.
Piper When the chips are down, always trust a chippie.
Brian I never get involved. It's asking for trouble, getting involved. You're into people's lives if you get involved. I've got enough troubles of my own.
Mark How is Peggy?
Brian What?
Piper Peggy.
Brian Still at her mother's. Still not coming to the phone. Still referring to me as "It".
Piper I should leave her if it was me.
Brian She's already left *me*, you breeze-block!
Mark (*standing*) Right. We'd better get up to The Manor.
Piper What's the rush?
Mark I just want to be gone, all right? (*He hesitates, wrestling with his conscience*) I ought to tell them.
Brian Ignorance is bliss.
Mark Not when you're having an extension done. (*He goes to knock at the door but stops*) What shall I say?
Piper Flannel.
Brian Or you could ... No — flannel.

Mark listens. There are no sounds of life from within the house

Mark No, we'll just go.
Brian Like thieves in the night.
Piper (*getting up*) I'll get our tools together.
Mark We don't need tools. It's just hanging a few tiles.
Piper Still ——
Mark No! Leave the tools. They won't feel so bad if we leave the tools.
Brian (*holding his sandwich up in front of his face*) Go on then. I'm not looking.
Mark Come on Piper.

They move to exit

Mary enters from the house with her shopping bag

Mary I'm just popping down to the village. Any special biscuits anyone likes?
Mark Oh. No no, anything will do.
Piper I'm rather partial to Ginger Nuts.

Mark shoots him a look

Mary Ginger Nuts. Right.

Mary exits happily R

Mark I'm going out on my own next year.
Brian Does your mother think you're old enough now then?
Mark I mean I'm going out on my own. I've had enough of mucking people about.
Brian You'll muck people about as well.
Mark Well, if I do — if I have to — at least I'll be honest with them.
Brian No, no, in the long run that's cruel. It's kinder to let them live in hope.
Piper Yes. Flannel.
Mark Like David, you mean?
Piper You've got to admit he's good at it.
Brian He's like a very skilled torturer he is. I mean, when he finally stops, most of his victims actually end up loving him.
Mark Well, when I go out on my own ——
Brian We'll all be old and grey.
Piper Or bald as a billiard-ball in your case.
Mark Yes, well, we'll see, won't we? Come on Piper.
Brian I'm not looking again.

Mark and Piper move to escape; they are foiled as ...

Jim enters from the house

Jim How's the coffee going, chaps? Like a top-up? Shall I put another jug on?
Piper Well ...
Mark No thanks, Mr Baxter.
Jim Fine. Whatever you like.
Mark Look Mr Baxter ...
Jim Yes?

Act I Scene 2

Mark As a matter of fact, me and Piper have got to go.
Jim Go? Go where?
Piper There's been an accident.
Mark No there hasn't. We've got to go up to The Manor. It's only for a couple of days.

Brian picks up his tools and exits quietly round the side of the house R

Jim But why?
Mark We're behind with the roof.
Jim No!
Mark No?
Jim Look, it's not fair. We haven't even got a roof.
Mark It will only be for a couple of days.
Piper Maybe just one.
Jim No. It's not fair.

David enters R. *Jim goes straight to him*

Jim It's not fair, David!
David What's that? What's not fair?
Jim They're going to The Manor.

David looks as if he is not best pleased with Mark for telling Jim

David (*to Jim*) Yes, I told you.
Jim You did not tell me!
David Are you sure? I'm sure I did.
Jim You did not tell me!
David Well, I certainly meant to. It's only for a couple of days.
Jim That isn't the point. They're ours!
David (*to Mark and Piper*) Would you mind, lads?

Mark and Piper are quite happy to withdraw. They exit L

Now look, Jim. I don't like splitting hairs because it's not in my nature, but this "Ours" business. It's not strictly true is it?
Jim No, of course it's not. But Mark and Piper have been with us from the start.
David Indeed they have. Every single day.

Jim That's what I'm saying.
David Even when we had the downpour. Remember them digging out the footings in that rain? Covered in clay, the pair of them.
Jim Yes, they were.
David I could have taken them away and put them on an inside job somewhere else, but I didn't.
Jim No you didn't, but ——
David They didn't thank me for keeping them here, you know.
Jim No I don't expect they did, but ——
David But here they stayed. "The Baxters are nice people," I said. I must have said that a dozen times that week with the rain pouring down. "The Baxters are nice people." Bucketing down it was.
Jim That was then.
David Quite right. That was then and this is now. But are you telling me honestly that you begrudge me borrowing them for a couple of days? Two little days?
Jim It's not a question of begrudging, David ...
David I apologize. I shouldn't have used the word. Only mean-spirited people begrudge things, in my experience. I apologize.
Jim That's all right.
David I mean, they're only on the path.
Jim It's not only a path. It's our path.
David And very nice it's looking too. They're matching the stones beautifully, aren't they?
Jim It's not only a path.
David Look Jim, I'll be totally honest with you. It's Ronnie Randall.
Jim What?
David You remember Ronnie.
Jim Oh yes. Nice chap.
David Nobody actually knows how old he is, you know. I don't think he knows himself. But for his age ... do you know, I often say to old Ronnie, "You'll see us all out, Ronnie." I often say that. But of course he won't. "Time and tide", and so on.
Jim What's wrong with him?
David Joints.
Jim Joints?
David Yes. Not his spirit, that's for sure. But his old joints ... well, he can't shin up and down a ladder like a young man any more. It stands to reason.
Jim He's doing the roof at The Manor isn't he?
David You've got it. He was decorated, you know. Royal Navy.

Act I Scene 2

Jim No, I didn't know.
David And seeing him up there, trying to finish off on his own ... As I say, he's got huge spirit. Huge spirit.
Jim But you've got other men.
David Not like Ronnie I haven't.
Jim I mean younger men. Men who *can* shin up and down ladders.

David gestures in the direction of Mark and Piper

Other men!
David I'm spread so thin, Jim, and that's the truth. I've got a barn conversion, the school roof—not your school. A dozen little jobs, all urgent—not that I think of little jobs as little jobs — another extension.
Jim Another extension?
David Yes. Just up the other side of the crossroads.
Jim Take their men!
David Jim, we're only six runs of bricks up and she's asthmatic.
Jim It's Mary, you see.
David Do you think I don't know that? I like women. I always have. But, bless their little hearts, when it comes to a situation like this, a practical situation, they do tend to make mountains out of mole-hills.
Jim No, that's not what I meant.
David What did you mean?
Jim Well she's had a lot to put up with, and I haven't been here and well — she's got more anger stored up than me.
David You're not saying she's taking it out on you?
Jim No.
David Because it's often the way.
Jim Is it?
David Oh yes. It's the different approach to things, you see. As I said, I like women, but it's emotion in everything, isn't it? It makes it difficult to get little things into perspective, sometimes. Emotion, emotion.
Jim (*blurting it out*) If only we could have a baby.
David Oh my dear chap! I am sorry. I didn't know.
Jim No, I mean it's not that we can't. No, physically it's all on. We just haven't been lucky.
David Now that explains a great deal to me, that does. I mean, wanting a baby — that's emotion on top of emotion, isn't it? Who could possibly blame her for not getting little things into perspective?
Jim You can't. No, you can't.

David After all, we are talking about a little thing. Losing Mark and Piper for just two days — it's not honestly a major setback, is it?
Jim It's a disappointment.
David A little blip, no more. Two days. What's two days?
Jim (*beaten*) I'll tell Mary about old Ronnie.
David In the strictest confidence, Jim. He's a proud man.
Jim Yes, of course.
David You hung the pheasants?
Jim The pheasants? Oh yes. Yes.
David That's the idea. I'm going shooting at the weekend. I'll bring you a rabbit or two.
Jim Thank you.
David You do like rabbit?
Jim (*obviously lying*) Oh yes. Very much. It *will* only be two days?
David Think of the relief old Ronnie's joints will get. Oh, some more good news. I did Charlie in the office an injustice. He hadn't forgotten the tiles. They are in hand.
Jim I thought Mary wanted to see a sample first.
David Did she? Right. Well you leave that with me. I'll go back and sort that out now. Oysters are very good, you know.
Jim Oysters?
David In a fertility sense.
Jim I thought they were just an aphrodisiac.
David That's only half the story, believe you me. I'll see if I can get you some. I've got a brother-in-law who's a fisherman. Oh, that's what I came round for. The new windows are in hand, well in hand.
Jim I'll tell Mary.
David That's the idea. Bye then Jim.
Jim Bye David.
David (*calling* L) Mark! Piper!
Mark
Piper } (*together, off*) Yes Boss?
David Come on! The sooner you're there, the sooner you're back!

Mark and Piper enter L, hurry past and exit R as they say the following

Mark
Piper } (*together*) Yes Boss!

David moves to follow Mark and Piper but then comes back to Jim

Act I Scene 2

David One more thing. Onions.
Jim Not like oysters?
David No, to go with the rabbit. I've got tons of them in the garden. I'll bring you some round.
Jim Thank you.

David puts an arm round Jim's shoulders and steers him back towards the house

David And don't worry. You'll have the baby.
Jim Yes, of course we will.
David That's the spirit. Bye Jim.
Jim Bye David.

Jim exits into the house and David shuts the door behind him

David heads for the exit R. The sound of sawing comes from inside the extension. David stops, moves to the foot of the ladder and whispers loudly up

David Brian?

The sawing noise stops and Brian appears on the scaffolding

Brian What?
David What are you doing here?
Brian The trusses.
David I told them you were sharpening your tools. I told them you'd be here tomorrow!
Brian Well I'm here today, so it doesn't really matter does it?
David Of course it matters! I don't want you here till next week.
Brian (*heading down the ladder*) Why tell them tomorrow then?
David To keep them happy.
Brian They're not happy.
David Look, where extensions are concerned, happiness is a comparative term.
Brian But I have actually finished at The Manor.
David I know that, but I've got Mrs Deakin on my back.
Brian She's a big woman too, Mrs Deakin.
David All right, Brian! The point is that you still haven't re-hung her doors.

Brian I didn't know I was supposed to.
David I had you down for that weeks ago.
Brian Well you didn't tell me.
David Are you sure?
Brian Positive.
David Well I can't go around telling everybody everything. Anyway, Mrs Deakin's got to be taken care of. She works for the Council, and you know what they can be like.
Brian Planning Department presumably?
David Exactly.
Brian Enough said. How many doors?
David All of them. It's looking more like the Leaning Tower of Pisa every day, that house. Well off you go then!
Brian I'll get my tools.

Brian goes back up the ladder to get his tools and exits into the extension

Mary enters R, carrying her shopping

David immediately tries to make his presence seem like good news

Mary Hallo David. Is everything all right?
David Oh yes, fine. I was just telling Jim that the new windows are in hand — well in hand. I was talking to Old Man Harper only half an hour ago.
Mary Oh good.
David Very secure they'll be. Very attractive too. Well, I must be off. Bye Mary.
Mary Goodbye David.

Brian comes down the ladder with his tools

Mary (*spotting him*) You've got your tools!

Brian guiltily drops his tool-bag

Mary David!
David Yes dear?

Brian picks up his tool-bag

Act I Scene 2

Mary Don't you "Dear" me! Where is he going? (*To Brian*) You stay where you are! Where is he going, David?

Brian drops his tool-bag again

David I just need to borrow him for a bit.
Mary What's he going to do, re-build Windsor Castle? (*To Brian*) You said you were staying!
Brian "So far as I'm concerned," I said.
Mary (*to David*) Well that brings it back to you, doesn't it?
David Which is only right and proper. I am where the buck stops and so on.
Mary So?
David Would you mind if Brian ... ?
Mary Yes I would!
David Well, would you mind if he just waited in the kitchen then?
Mary Very well.
David Brian!

Brian picks up his tool-bag, edges warily round Mary and exits into the house

Right Mary, now the thing is this ——
Mary No. The thing is this. I've had it with excuses. I don't want to listen to any more excuses!
David I see. Well that sort of cuts the ground from under my feet doesn't it?
Mary Which was exactly my intention. It's your firm, David. You take him away. You put him on some other job and tell me that he'll be back tomorrow or the day after or the week after. Just take him. But don't insult my intelligence any further by explaining *why* you're taking him by giving me a load of pure bullshit!
David May I ask you a question?
Mary (*cautiously*) Yes.
David Would you call Doctor Ringwood an inveterate liar?
Mary Of course I wouldn't. What are you talking about?
David Ring him up and ask him to verify little Naomi's ears. (*He calls*) Brian!

Brian comes to the kitchen doorway

Brian Hallo?

David Did or did not Ronnie's cat get under the floorboards at The Manor?
Brian Yes it did. It was funny actually because ——
Mary I withdraw bullshit.
David Thank you.
Mary Not at all.

Brian decides he will be safer in the kitchen and goes back in

David Now as to an *explanation*, Mary, I'm going to have to confide in you. I hope you can keep a secret. I'm sure you can. It is absolutely imperative that Brian re-hangs Mrs Deakin's doors a.s.a.p. and then some.
Mary Why ... I don't ... why should that be a secret?
David She works in the Council Offices. In the Planning Department.
Mary Well, it's not MI5 is it?
David *And* Mary, *and* — if she isn't kept sweet, she can influence things. Do you get my drift?
Mary We've already got planning permission.
David Not for that extra little dormer window you decided on.
Mary (*looking up; this is obviously a weak spot*) It's just a little window.
David A little window not covered by the original planning permission.
Mary She couldn't say "No".
David Couldn't she?
Mary It's blackmail!
David I'm not blackmailing you, Mary.
Mary No. This Mrs Deakin. She's blackmailing you.
David And I'm prepared to let her do it for your sake. It's up to you, Mary.
Mary How long will it take Brian?
David No time at all. He could be back here by tomorrow.
Mary All right David. Take Brian.
David Think of your little dormer window.
Mary Yes.
David (*calling*) Brian!

Brian appears in the kitchen doorway with a cup of tea and a piece of cake

Brian Hallo?
David Come on. We're going now.

Disappointed, Brian puts down the tea and cake, picks up his tool-bag and comes out

Act I Scene 2

Mary See you tomorrow Brian.
Brian So far as I'm concerned.
David (*hustling Brian towards the exit* R) Bye then Mary.
Mary Bye David.

David and Brian exit R

Jim appears in the kitchen, but, seeing Mary, he retreats into the house

Mary heads for the back door, but changes her mind and sits on one of the garden chairs

Jim comes round the side of the house L *carrying a children's text book and quite plainly expecting that Mary has now gone into the house*

Jim Oh you're back. (*He holds up the book*) I thought I'd do a bit of work in the garden.
Mary Good idea.
Jim (*sitting*) I washed up the coffee things.
Mary Good.
Jim (*welling up to a confession*) Mary...
Mary I let David take Brian away!

There is a pause. Mary is obviously waiting for an explosion

Jim I see.
Mary It's our extra little dormer window. If he doesn't do something to some woman's doors, she'll turn down our application because she works at the Council Offices. It'll only be for a day. I didn't know what else to do.
Jim It's all right, love. You didn't have much choice, did you?
Mary Well no.
Jim So that's all there is to it. Don't worry.
Mary If you'd let David take Brian away an hour after he arrived, I'd have hit the roof. Ha! The roof!
Jim It's as I keep saying. We couldn't expect a totally smooth passage with an extension. There's no such thing.
Mary (*putting her hand on his arm*) It's David. When he's not here, I think of all the right things to say, like working out chess moves in advance. But then you make your opening gambit and suddenly you're playing draughts instead. And he's so convincing. His reasons always seem so ... so reasonable.

Jim That's because they are really.

Mary Perhaps I should have given him more of an argument.

Jim You said yourself that getting your little dormer window depended on it.

Mary That's true.

Jim And you know, I don't think David's always flannelling for the sake of flannelling. He's not actually a dishonest man.

Mary Naomi really did have a problem with her ears — and the cat did get under the floorboards.

Jim Well there you are. I know his excuses reach *War and Peace* lengths sometimes, but in the end you do have to believe them.

Mary Yes you do.

Jim Like old Ronnie Randall.

Mary What about Ronnie Randall?

Jim Well, his age.

Mary I'm not with you.

Jim Well we had him here for those three days, didn't we? With the best will in the world you couldn't call him sprightly. And when you think of old Ronnie trying to finish off the roof-tiles at The Manor ... He was decorated, you know. I didn't know that.

Mary gets up suddenly as if an awful suspicion has dawned on her. She goes round the side of the house R

Jim Where are you going? (*He knows, of course, and waits for her to reappear*)

Mary enters R and looks off R towards the gate

Mary They've gone! Mark and Piper have gone!

Jim Yes I know. That's what I was trying to tell you.

Mary You let David take Mark and Piper.

Jim It's only for a couple of days.

Mary Oh Jim! Why?

Jim Old Ronnie Randall.

Mary Look, if he's that decrepit, he shouldn't be working at all. It's not our business.

Jim I think "decrepit" is a bit harsh.

Mary They were our one constant, Mark and Piper — our one lifeline.

Jim They were only on the path.

Mary It's not "only!" Why does everyone keep saying, "It's only a path"?

Act I Scene 2

Jim Because it is. They can finish that off anytime. Mark said last week that there wasn't anything to be getting on with until Brian arrived.
Mary Brian did arrive!
Jim Yes — and then you let him go.
Mary Oh I see.
Jim Well you did.
Mary Yes I did. And what did you say? "It's all right, love," you said, "you didn't have much choice, did you?" That's what you said.
Jim And I meant it.
Mary No you didn't. You were just preparing the ground before telling me what a wimp you'd been!
Jim I wondered when we'd get to "wimp".
Mary I've never used that expression before.
Jim No. But now you've started, it's going to become your buzz word, isn't it?
Mary Oh don't be silly!
Jim Well that's the end of seaside holidays. It stands to reason doesn't it? "Oh look, there's a wimp. Kick sand in his face!"
Mary Oh that's pathetic! Old Ronnie Randall!
Jim Why are we back on old Ronnie Randall?
Mary Because that's a pathetic excuse and you swallowed it.
Jim At least we've seen him. At least we've seen him struggling about. I don't remember seeing this woman who works for the Council who has the power of life and death over your little dormer window!
Mary You're back-tracking. You have to see excuses now, is that the new rule? Exhibit A! Exhibit B! Why don't you go round to Charlie's house and peer into his daughter's ears if it will make you feel any better?
Jim Who says this woman has the power of life and death anyway?
Mary She works for the Planning Department!
Jim For all you know, she might clean the lavatories.

There is a pause

Mary That's — that's ——
Jim And you *don't* know do you?
Mary No, all right. I don't.
Jim Then don't be so quick to jump down my throat!
Mary I'm entitled to jump where I like! "I'm home for the school holidays," you said. You made it sound like the relief of Mafeking! "Leave it all to me," you said, and the first thing you do is lose two-thirds of our workforce!

Jim Well I certainly wouldn't have let Brian go.
Mary No? You'd have probably carried his tool-bag for him!
Jim You know what you're turning into don't you? A shrew!
Mary As in *The Taming of* ... ?
Jim Yes. All the time. Every hour of every day you're on and on and on.
Mary I have to go on and on and on.
Jim Yes, but not at me!
Mary You don't seem to realize what sort of state my nerves are in.
Jim Oh I do. I do.
Mary You must have a little door in your brain that you can just close and lock. I can't! It's on my mind all the time!
Jim Don't I know it? No wonder we're not having a baby!
Mary What?
Jim You're not making love to me any more. You're making love to a builders' manual. All you're thinking about is trusses and joists and breeze blocks!
Mary And who are you making love to? Me or some tart in a black suspender belt? The next thing you'll want is scenery and a full orchestra!

They both look hurt

Oh God, I'm sorry. I didn't mean it.
Jim I didn't mean it.

Both upset, they fall into each other's arms

Mary It's this bloody extension. It's been going on so long. I can't remember a time when it hasn't been going on.
Jim I know. It's us, isn't it? We've started taking it out on each other.
Mary We said we'd never do that.
Jim That was a rotten thing I said about the baby — a really bloody rotten stinking thing.
Mary Oh you may be right.
Jim No.
Mary I'm so tense all the time. I don't mind wearing a suspender belt for you.
Jim I shouldn't ask you. It's so bloody infantile.
Mary It's not. I don't mind. I like it.
Jim Do you really?
Mary Yes.
Jim You don't really feel like a tart?
Mary Of course not. Look, is there anything else?

Act I Scene 2

Jim What?
Mary I don't know. Anything else.
Jim No. Is there anything I'm not doing? I mean, if there is ...
Mary You're lovely.
Jim Oh yes, I'm lovely all right.
Mary You are.
Jim Listen and re-think. Do you know what I did today? I betrayed you, that's what I did.
Mary Oh come on. How?
Jim With David. I told him about us wanting a baby and not ... not being lucky.
Mary Oh. Well that's not betraying me is it?
Jim Yes it is, because I let him use it. I stood there and allowed him to accept the man-to-man inference. You know, "The little woman at a time like this. Bound to over-react." All that. It's like *Nineteen Eighty-Four* isn't it? "Have a good day and betray somebody!"
Mary Well, "Snap" then. Weeks ago I told him that I had to have all the rows because you didn't have the back-bone.

Jim turns away thoughtfully as if taking this in; then he suddenly turns back to Mary

Jim Go away.
Mary What?
Jim Go away. Get out of it for a bit.
Mary What would you do?
Jim Stay here.
Mary Where would I go?
Jim I don't know. Your mother's. Go to your mother's.
Mary She'd drive me mad. I mean, really mad.
Jim A hotel then.
Mary We can't afford a hotel.
Jim I don't care! It would just get you out of it. It would get one of us out of it.
Mary (*getting upset*) No! I can't leave you here. It's got to be us here — it's for *us*! (*She starts to cry*) I don't want to go away. I want to stay here with you!
Jim Oh don't cry, love. Please don't cry!

They hug, but as they find solace in each other's arms, Jim starts to cry as well

CURTAIN

ACT II

Scene 1

A month later

The large truss has now gone. Slates and various items of a new bathroom suite, including a bath and a sink unit, lie around the grass. There are intermittent sounds of hammering and sawing from inside the extension

Mark, in shorts, enters R carrying a new toilet. He rests

Piper, also in shorts, comes on from the garden and woods L

Piper There's six dead pheasants and four dead rabbits down the woods.
Mark They're chucking them away as fast as David gives them to them.
Piper Why not just say they don't want them?
Mark Why do you always go down the woods to pee anyway?
Piper I don't like peeing in other people's houses.
Mark It's not another allergy is it?
Piper I just don't feel comfortable.
Mark You poop down there as well, don't you?
Piper Sometimes.
Mark Disgusting. Come on, give us a hand.
Piper I resent this.
Mark I thought you might.
Piper I'm a brickie, not a plumber's labourer.
Mark Look, the bathroom suite's been delivered. We can't leave it out here, can we?
Piper That's Dino's job, isn't it?
Mark He's not here, is he?
Piper Living it up on the Via Veneto, I suppose.
Mark He's only one sixteenth Italian. He's never even been to Italy.
Piper Hey, I have. I went to the World Cup, didn't I?
Mark Yes — for two days. Then you got deported.
Piper They don't know how to take a joke, that's their trouble. Bloody unreasonable.

Act II Scene 1

Mark picks up a sink unit and climbs the ladder; the following conversation takes place as he ascends, puts the unit into the extension and descends again

Mark Look, I'll take this up. Do you want to get the bidet?
Piper No I don't.
Mark Well get it anyway.
Piper I don't see Brian helping.
Mark He's doing the studwork.
Piper Oh pardon me for asking. I mean, that's the equivalent of splitting the atom, isn't it?
Mark You know what your trouble is, don't you? You're demarcation mad.
Piper There's nothing wrong with a bit of demarcation. People doing the job they're supposed to, that's what it means.
Mark That's all yesterday.
Piper More's the pity. (*He sits on the toilet bowl*) I mean, look what's happened to sex.
Mark Sex?
Piper Yes.
Mark Without demarcation?
Piper Yes.
Mark When did sex ever have demarcation?
Piper When things were *right*. Look at it now. Who knows who's who any more? There's women acting like men. There's men acting like women. Total confusion. Confusion about who has the right to be on top in bed. Confusion as to who is supposed to say they want to be on top. There's women faking orgasms while they think about what to cook for next night's dinner. Then there's the "New Man," trying so hard to prolong the pleasure for his partner that he tries to name all the kings and queens of England in the right order instead of just getting on with it. The result? No-one knows who's supposed to be pleasing who any more, so nobody's really being pleased at all. And why? No demarcation!
Mark Are you still going out with that girl from the chemist's?
Piper She's got nothing to do with it!
Mark You're just generalizing then?
Piper All right, a particular. I'll give you a particular. (*He points to the house*) Them in there. They're confused.
Mark Of course they are. They're having an extension.
Piper All right, yes. But here's the *abnormal* confusion. Who should be up the front when it comes to trying to get some sense out of David?

Mark Well, he should, I suppose.
Piper Right. And who is up the front?
Mark Well, she is mostly.
Piper Exactly!
Mark Was.
Piper What?
Mark She was up the front. The last few weeks neither of them have been up the front.
Piper That's true.
Mark They've gone very quiet. No sign of the famous tiles from Germany.
Piper David's probably got some old peasant wheeling them across Europe in a wheelbarrow.
Mark Plumber a week late. No plasterers, no electricians. And not a word.
Piper If they knew who was who ...
Mark No, it's not that. I think their spirits are broken. Does she insist on being on top then?
Piper Who, Mrs Baxter?
Mark The girl from the chemist's.
Piper It's none of your business is that.
Mark Get the bidet.
Piper Under protest.
Mark Whatever.
Piper I wouldn't let a girl insist anyway.
Mark Oh I see.
Piper And *that's* demarcation!

Piper exits triumphantly R

Mark shakes his head, picks up the toilet bowl and starts up the ladder. As he does so ...

Brian appears through the extension window and comes down the ladder

Mark descends and waits for him

Brian Now that's well-timed. I just wanted to go.
Mark Why does sanitary-ware always produce sanitary-ware jokes?
Brian It's obvious.
Mark That's what I mean.
Brian It's about tea-time isn't it?

Act II Scene 1   41

Mark Should be.

Mark takes the toilet bowl on up the ladder and sets it on the scaffolding

Brian No sign of Dino then?
Mark Of course not. All his units are here, all his piping. Everything's ready to go. Why on earth should he be here?

Mark gets some more sanitary-ware on to the scaffolding

Piper enters R carrying a bidet

Piper I don't know why people have bidets. They're just status symbols.
Brian Wonder they don't wear them round their necks really.
Piper Do you want to give us a hand with this?
Brian No thanks.
Piper Chain-saw Chippie!

Brian sits down. Piper goes up the ladder and hands the bidet to Mark who sets it down on the scaffolding

Jim enters from the house with a tray on which there are mugs, milk, sugar and biscuits

Jim Tea up, lads!
Mark ⎫
Piper ⎬ (*together*) Thank you Mr Baxter.
Brian ⎭

Jim sets the tray down

Jim How's the studding going then, Brian?
Brian That's studwork.
Jim Yes. Sorry. How's that going then?
Brian I'll be plaster-boarding soon.
Jim That's pretty good, isn't it?
Brian At the risk of sounding immodest, it's phenomenal.
Jim Excellent. Concentrate on the good things, that's the trick.
Brian Is it?
Jim Oh yes. Concentrate on the good things.

Jim exits into the house

Mark and Piper join Brian

Piper Good-oh. Ginger Nuts.
Mark I should put in for some smoked salmon sandwiches for tomorrow.

Mary enters from the house with the teapot. She seems subdued in a dreamy sort of way

Mary Here we are.
Mark
Piper } (*together*) Thank you Mrs Baxter.
Brian
Mary Everything all right?
Mark
Piper } (*together*) Fine. Fine.
Brian
Mary That's good. That's good, isn't it?

She exits into the house

Mark See what I mean? That's not just quiet. That's peculiar quiet.
Brian There's a reason for that. She's been on tranquillizers for the last few weeks.
Mark How do you know that?
Brian (*pointing to the scaffolding*) Sound travels upwards.
Mark No it doesn't.

During the following, Brian pours the tea. All that comes out of the teapot is hot water

Brian Well I heard them talking about it anyway. It was his idea in the first place. He said —— (*He breaks off*) She's given us hot water.
Piper (*calling*) Mrs Baxter!
Mark She's not the maid. Go in!

Piper moves towards the back door with the teapot. Mary enters and meets him

Mary Did somebody call?

Act II Scene 1

Piper There's no tea in the teapot.

Mary frowns, lifts the lid off the teapot, then giggles

Mary That's silly, isn't it. Sorry. Oh dear. (*She makes as if to go back in the house with just the lid of the teapot*)
Piper Mrs Baxter.

Mary giggles again, puts the lid on the teapot and takes it from Piper

Mary Sorry.

Mary exits into the house, still giggling

Mark My God, look what we've done to her!
Piper It's not our fault.
Brian I hope she doesn't get addicted.
Mark Oh come on, they wouldn't be that strong.
Brian Depends what they are. A woman over Chiddingfold way was totally dependent on them by the time we fitted her kitchen.
Mark Oh dear.
Piper It's not our fault.
Mark He never asks me how I got on at cricket any more.
Piper There's not much point. You never get any runs.
Mark I mean, he's not on tranquillizers as well is he?
Brian No, only her. He's just keeping his head down. "Concentrate on the good things," that's his new motto.
Piper How come you're such a mine of information?
Brian I've got the sort of face that makes people want to talk to me.

Piper stares at Brian's face and shakes his head

Mark What good things? What good things has he got to concentrate on?
Brian Well, there's me for a start.
Mark That *is* stretching the imagination.
Brian No it's not. He's felted and battened. I'm well on with the studwork.
Piper Yes, it's not as though things have ground to a halt is it?
Mark They soon will. We've crashed on the beach. How long is he going to have to wait for the next wave?

Their reaction shows that they all see the truth in this

Piper There was talk of old Ronnie Randall coming round to help us with the roof tiles.
Mark He's not a wave. He's not even a ripple.

Jim enters from the house with the teapot

Jim Sorry about that lads. I think we got it right this time.
Mark
Piper } (*together*) Thank you Mr Baxter.
Brian

Jim exits into the house

Brian What's the betting he's given us Lucozade?

Brian pours. It is tea; they give a little cheer. Piper takes his tea over to the bench, sets it down and starts to chalk on a piece of slate

Mark What are you doing?
Piper Well, I'm not writing a novel am I?

The other two join him on the bench

Piper I'm trying to work out old Ronnie Randall's age. Now he's always saying he remembers the Kaiser. So when was the Kaiser?

They all give this thought with no result

David enters R

David (*pointing behind him*) I shouldn't leave that bath up there, Mark. You know what people are like.
Mark Right-ho, Boss.

David knocks on the back door

David Anybody home?

Act II Scene 1

Brian That's debatable really.

Jim and Mary enter from the house

Jim Hallo David.
David Hallo Jim. Hallo Mary. Did you enjoy the rabbit over the weekend?
Jim Oh yes.
Mary Yes we did.
Jim We boiled it.
Mary That's it.
Jim With herbs.
Piper (*looking down the garden*) Wild herbs.
David Jolly good, jolly good. Well we're coming along at a pace now, aren't we? It's starting to look like a house again.
Mary Like a house again.
Jim No news on the plumber, I suppose?
David Oh he's imminent. And your floor tiles for the hall are definitely in this country.
Jim You said that on Friday.
David Ah. And you're wondering why they're not actually here yet?
Jim More or less.
David Now there's a very interesting story attached to that.

Behind David, on the bench, Mark, Piper and Brian all cross their knees and wait to hear what David is going to come up with this time

You see, they got to Dover all right. They were in a container with some other goods from Germany you see. Well, you know what it's like these days, with drugs coming in from all over the place. So they had sniffer dogs sniff at the containers. Well when they got to the one with your tiles in, they went mad apparently.

Jim Tiles don't smell, do they?
David You've got to remember that I said there were lots of other goods in that container — all sorts of things. Any old how, the Customs and Excise boys had no alternative but to inspect the container. And where would be whatever was driving the dogs mad? Right at the back!

During the following, Mark, Piper and Brian all copy David's gestures and mouth the words

Well of course the Customs and Excise boys had no alternative but to unpack the whole container. And do you know what was driving those dogs mad?
Jim No.
Mary No.
David Aftershave!

Behind David, Piper produces three pieces of slate. He and the other lads start to write on them with chalk

David There were two cases of aftershave and one of the bottles had broken — faulty packing. Not like the Germans. They're very thorough people as a rule.
Jim Why would aftershave smell like drugs?
David You tell me, but it did to the dogs. Of course they had the stuff analysed and gave it a clean bill of health. But here's the point. I've got a great deal of time for the Customs and Excise boys. I mean, most of them will turn a blind eye to the odd bottle over your allowance, of course they will. But I suppose it's only human nature to prefer unpacking a container when you think you're on to something than re-packing it when you know you're not.
Jim So our tiles ... ?
David You've got it, Jim. In the country, as I said, but stuck at Dover for a bit.

Behind David, the lads hold up their pieces of slate like gymnastics judges. Each slate has a big "10" chalked on it. Jim and Mary giggle involuntarily

It is a funny story isn't it? (*He looks round*)

The lads hide the slates. Inside the house the telephone rings

Jim Phone. I'll go.

Jim exits into the house

David If that's the Harrises ringing round, I'm on my way.
Jim (*off*) Right.
David Well lads, I'm not clock-watching, but ...

Mark, Piper and Brian take the hint and start to go back to work

Act II Scene 1   47

Mark and Piper exit towards the gate R

Brian starts to climb the ladder to the scaffolding

Mary You won't have time for a cup of tea then, David?
David I'd love one to tell you the truth Mary, but if it is the Harrises ... he's an airline pilot, you see.

Jim enters from the house with a portable telephone

Jim It's for you, Brian.
Brian Me?
Jim It's your wife.

Looking suspicious, Brian comes down the ladder and takes the telephone

Brian Hallo? ... What? ... When? ... No, of course I'll come with you. I'll leave now. ... Yes, look, try not to get into a state. (*He hands the phone to Jim, looking very worried*) I'll have to go. They've found a lump. They're going to take a bit of tissue.
David Oh my dear old boy, you get off.
Jim Yes of course, Brian. Go on.
Mary You look after her.
Brian Yes. I'll get off then.

Brian takes out his car keys and exits R

Piper (*off*) Knocking off already? Where are you going, Ascot?
David I think I will have that cup of tea now, Mary, if you don't mind.
Mary Yes. I'll get a cup.

Mary exits into the house

David sits down

Jim That's awful.
David You never know, do you?
Jim No, you don't.

Mark and Piper enter R *carrying a new bath*

Piper I didn't know, did I?
Mark You didn't even notice the expression on his face!

They take the bath into the house, passing Mary as she enters with a cup for David

Mary pours David's tea

David Thank you Mary.
Jim It could be benign. It's a biopsy, isn't it? That's what it's called.
David A "Yes" or a "No". Who'd be a woman, eh?
Jim Are you all right, love?
Mary Yes, just a bit tired.

Mary takes the portable phone from Jim and exits into the house

David I'll tell Brian to stop hammering. Oh, no need.

Jim sits down

"In the midst of life" and so on, eh?
Jim Right out of the blue.
David Do you know Fred Curle?
Jim Fred Curle? I don't think so.
David You must know him. He does a bit of gardening for people. Always rides his old bike — a big old stand-up job. You must know him.
Jim I've probably seen him.
David You're bound to have. Very useful fast bowler when he was young. Used to play for the village.
Jim Did he?
David Only trouble with Fred was that he used to get very moody if he wasn't put on to bowl down the slope.
Jim Really? Why did you mention him?
David He died last Friday.
Jim Oh.
David Working at the Gladstone place; he was cutting the hedge. He wasn't discovered till Mr Gladstone came home from work in the evening. Just lying there. He still had his shears in his hands. Gone — just like that. Nice high bowling action he had, Fred Curle.

Act II Scene 1

Jim You said the plumber was imminent?

David Oh yes. Then there was Jack Topley. He was taken a month ago. Only forty-five. Collapsed in the *King's Arms*. He'd just had a lot of fillings done as well.

Jim He didn't work for you did he?

David Jack Topley? Good heavens no. He was a postman. Why do you ask?

Jim I wondered if you were leading up to something.

David No, no. Just chatting about "In the midst of life" and so on.

Jim Because, you see ...

David To tell the truth, Jim, I haven't been feeling too well myself lately.

Jim Oh?

David No. It's hard to put your finger on it. I don't know, just a bit out of sorts — a bit tired I suppose.

Jim You are leading up to something!

David Now what could I possibly be leading up to?

Jim I don't know, David. I'm not in your class, I've come to realize that, but ... the plumber! That's what you're leading up to! You've used old Ronnie Randall's health and now you're using yours. Somehow, somehow, it's going to have something to do with us not getting a plumber for the next six weeks!

David I don't say this lightly Jim, but that isn't worthy of you.

Jim Isn't it?

David No it's not.

Jim Well if I'm wrong, I'm sorry.

David Thank you.

Jim Another cup of tea?

David No thanks, no. I'd better be getting over to the Harrises in a minute.

David suddenly moves his rump as if in pain

Jim What's the matter?

David Sitting on some coins.

Jim Oh.

David Well, how's Mary then? No sign of any ... ? (*He makes gestures towards his own stomach*)

Jim No.

David Bad luck that. Still, she's looking very well in herself.

Jim You think so?

David Oh yes. More relaxed in herself too. She seems to be taking the whole business more in her stride now.

Jim She's on tranquillizers.

David Oh. Didn't know that. Still, as I said before, a woman's emotional reactions ——

Jim No, not again, David! I'm not using her as an excuse for all the things that I don't do.

David What things?

Jim Where do I start? Just putting up with it all. Not making more of a fuss.

David Jim, you don't want to rant and scream every time I come round here. You don't want a continual shouting match. It's not your way, Jim. It never will be.

Jim No, it's not my way.

David And thank the Lord for that. A man doesn't respect another man for doing that sort of thing, and it doesn't get you anywhere in the end. It just creates bad feeling and high blood pressure.

Jim I'm not good at being angry, you see. Some people are. They can *act* angry without ever really getting angry. I can't do that.

David And who would want you to? I wouldn't. Your Mary wouldn't.

Jim I'm not so sure sometimes.

David No, Jim, you leave the shouters of this world to their own devices. How long have you been down here now — eight years?

Jim Five.

David Five — and do you know something? You're *liked* — genuinely liked. Not many people can really claim that, can they?(*He gets up*) I hope it's all right with Brian's missis. They haven't had an easy ride you know. Well, I must get along to the Harrises — he's an airline pilot you know. And then — and this is a solemn promise, Jim — I'll get on to the Customs and Excise boys at Dover about your tiles. Bye Jim.

Jim (*getting up*) Bye David.

David makes as if to go, then comes back to Jim

David Oh, and don't think I've forgotten.

Jim The gatepost?

David No, the oysters. I just haven't been down that way recently. Bye!

David exits R

Jim, as usual, is left feeling that he hasn't won a single point. He sits down. The telephone rings inside the house. Jim gets up to answer it, but it stops ringing; Mary has obviously answered it. Jim sits down again

Act II Scene 2

Mary enters slowly from the house. She looks shell-shocked

Jim Mary?
Mary That was Doctor Ringwood. I'm pregnant.
Jim (*getting up*) But you didn't even say——
Mary I couldn't. I couldn't raise your hopes again. We're going to have a baby!
Jim (*taking Mary in his arms*) We're going to have a baby!

They scream with sheer excitement

Mark and Piper enter from the house, looking worried

Mark Are you all right?
Jim All right? All right? We're going to have a baby!

Mark and Piper cheer. Piper motions Mark towards the pieces of slate they left by the bench. Mark understands and they each hold aloft a "10"

Touched, Jim and Mary exit into the house

Mark Nice gesture that, Piper. They were so excited, weren't they?
Piper Yes. Bit over the top, really, though. I mean, it has been done before, hasn't it?

CURTAIN

SCENE 2

The same. The following day

From inside the extension comes the magic sound of fourteen people at work. There are the noises of hammering, sawing, drilling, etc.

Jim and Mary enter R; Mary carries shopping and Jim a large teddy bear

Mary I thought everybody knew Fred Curle. You must have seen him around.
Jim Perhaps I didn't take him in.
Mary Well it's too late now.

Jim Yes. Funny name, Curle. Probably derived from ... (*suddenly*) Listen!

They stop

Mary What?
Jim The noise! Listen!
Mary It's just building noise. You go through a tolerance barrier, then it just becomes like musak.
Jim I'm talking about the volume. Even if Brian's back, three men can't produce that volume of noise — that *variety* of noise! Listen!

Mary looks as if she realizes there is some truth in what Jim is saying. Excitedly, Jim climbs part way up the ladder and looks over the edge of the scaffolding. His eyes widen and he hurries back down the ladder

Jim There's hundreds of them! No, not hundreds, that's silly. But a lot. There are a lot of people in there and they're working on *our* extension!
Mary It's all coming right.
Jim Yes. Everything's coming right!

Mary exits into the house with the shopping

Jim hugs the teddy bear in sheer joy

Piper enters R with some plumbing equipment and sees Jim with the teddy bear

Jim It's for the baby.
Piper I thought it might be, yes. (*He starts to go up the ladder*)
Jim Piper — all these people?
Piper (*stopping*) Half the work-force you've got here.
Jim (*impressed*) Half?
Piper You've even got Dino, and he's like gold-dust.
Jim Dino?
Piper The plumber.

Piper carries on up the scaffolding and exits into the extension

Jim (*shouting excitedly into the house*) Mary! We've got a plumber — a real live plumber!

Act II Scene 2

From inside the house we hear a squeal of delight from Mary

Mark enters R

Mark Good-morning, Mr Baxter.
Jim (*shaking Mark's hand effusively*) Good-morning Mark. Good-morning! It's all coming right!
Mark (*a little guiltily*) Yes, that's the idea. Well —— (*He starts up the ladder*)
Jim Oh Mark, I should have thought. Any news from Brian — about his wife?
Mark (*stopping*) Not yet, no. It's all right though. Biggles is here.
Jim Biggles?
Mark The other carpenter.
Jim The other carpenter. My God!
Mark Yes — and now Dino's here we can start carcassing in.
Jim Can you? That's incredible! What's carcassing in?
Mark Laying down cables and pipes. You know — water and lights.
Jim Water and lights! Now this is really getting on, isn't it?
Mark A "Blitz", that's what we call this. We get in each other's way a bit, but it doesn't half shift things along. A bit noisy though.
Jim We don't mind the noise. We *like* the noise! "Carcassing in!"

Mark continues on up the ladder and exits into the extension

Mary enters from the house with a can of lager for Jim and a can of soft drink for herself

They'll be carcassing in soon.
Mary Will they? What's that?
Jim Oh, laying down the pipes and cables — for water and lights ...
Mary Funny expression — "carcassing in".
Jim They do have some funny expressions.
Mary They're not pulling our legs are they? I mean, that isn't some subtle allusion to those pheasants and rabbits we've been chucking away? You know — carcasses.
Jim No. They don't know they're there do they? I mean, they don't have any reason to go down the woods. Oh who cares anyway? (*He kisses Mary happily*)

A cheer goes up from above

Some of them are on the roof. Do you realize what I just said? "Some of them are on the roof!" It's got a ring to it, hasn't it?

Mary A peal!

They sip their drinks

(*Suddenly thoughtful*) Why, though? Why are there suddenly so many people here?

Jim Mark says it's called a "Blitz".

Mary I don't mind what it's called. I want to know why. What's David up to?

Jim Well if you must know, I had a bit of a go at him.

Mary Oh?

Jim Well, not so much a go. I simply pointed out that I wasn't falling for any line about him not feeling well.

Mary When did he say he wasn't feeling well?

Jim Before I had a go at him. In fact, I suggested that he was preparing the ground to make some excuse about not looking after us properly.

Mary Good for you.

Jim I didn't shout.

Mary No. What did he say?

Jim He said a suggestion like that wasn't worthy of me.

Mary My God! He's the one to talk.

Jim I must have hit a nerve though. Why else a "Blitz"? They could be finished in a couple of weeks.

Mary Yes. More good news for Mum tonight. You don't mind staying over, do you? It's better than having to drive back, isn't it?

Jim The way I feel at the moment, I'm even quite fond of her. We'll leave the key with Mark so they can all get in in the morning. All get in!

Mary She is thrilled about the baby. To her way of thinking, I'm finally giving her a grandson.

Jim I don't mind if it's a girl, you know.

Mary Perhaps we'll have one of each now we've got the knack.

Jim It wasn't the tranquilizers was it?

Mary No. Pre-tranquillizers. It must have been just after we cried.

Jim I felt a fool.

Mary You shouldn't. Personally, I think it was the Dance of The Seven Veils that did it.

Jim I don't know why I did that. I don't know what got into me.

Act II Scene 2

Mary You were very good. Did you mean to throw your pants through the window?
Jim No, I just got carried away.
Mary I'm glad you remembered to pop out and get them back. I think the lads' tongues might have wagged if they'd found them.
Jim We did laugh.
Mary Yes, we did.
Jim Perhaps that's the secret, laughing. Perhaps if we go for another I should go the whole hog and hire a funny costume.
Mary Let's have this one first.
Jim Yes. This one.
Mary The baby was the talisman!
Jim What?
Mary We built the extension for the baby and now the baby has made this happen! It has!
Jim Perhaps you're right. Either way, it's all coming true.
Mary Yes, it's all coming true. I'd better make the lads some tea. How many are there exactly?
Jim I'll ask.

Mary exits into the house

(*Shouting up at the scaffolding*) Mark!

Mark enters, climbing out onto the scaffolding

Mark Yes, Mr Baxter?
Jim How many for tea?
Mark Just a minute.(*He looks inside the extension and does a head count*) Fourteen, please. Biggles says he'd like a champagne cocktail, but ignore him.
Jim Fourteen teas. Right. (*He heads toward the back door, quite emotional*) Did you hear that Mary? Fourteen teas!

He exits

CURTAIN

Scene 3

The following day

There are no sounds of massed workmen

There is the sound of a car approaching and pulling up

Piper emerges quickly from the extension and heads towards the woods, L

Piper I'm just going for a pee.

Mark sticks his head out of a window in the extension

Mark That's all very convenient isn't it?
Piper It's Nature. Nature calls. What can I do about it?
Mark Put it off.
Piper No way.

Piper heads towards the exit L

Mark enters from the extension

Mark Piper!

But Piper exits L

We hear Jim and Mary approaching R

Mark ducks round the corner of the house L, *as Jim and Mary enter* R *carrying overnight bags*

Jim I mean, Jason!
Mary It was only a suggestion.
Jim The trouble with your mother's suggestions are that they ultimately assume the proportions of a Papal Bull.
Mary I'm not keen on it.
Jim I hate it.
Mary Perhaps "Something" Jason?
Jim Jason Jason, how about that?

Act II Scene 3

Mary If it's a girl, we could call her Jasonette.

They laugh but are jarred into silence by the lack of noise from the house

Mary It's quiet isn't it?
Jim Yes. Perhaps they're all ...
Mary Perhaps they're all what?
Jim Doing something quiet?

It is obvious that neither of them believes this

Mark! Mark!

Mark slides on to the patio L as if he has been grouting the bricks all along

Mark Good-morning. Have a nice time?
Jim Yes thank you. Where is everybody?
Mark Piper's about somewhere.
Jim I mean "Everybody".
Mark Ah.
Mary Oh Mark!
Mark I wasn't told. I just turned up.
Mary That bloody David!

She exits into the house

Jim None of you care do you? None of you *really* care.

Jim follows Mary into the house

Piper enters cautiously from the woods L

Piper How did they take it?
Mark Do you really care how they took it?
Piper No.
Mark Oh sweet!
Piper What do you want me to do, burst into tears?
Mark You might show a little sympathy.
Piper Like you?
Mark Yes.
Piper So what are you *doing* about it?

Mark When I go out on my own ——
Piper Yes, we know. You'll be the Mother Theresa of the building trade.
Mark At least I'll try.
Piper So what's stopping you?

Mary and Jim enter from the house

Mary If he's not round here in five minutes like I said, I'm cancelling the contract!
Jim We haven't got a contract.
Mary I don't care! I'm cancelling it!
Jim We feel very let down about this.
Piper You would.
Mark You're entitled.
Mary To an explanation?
Mark Yes.
Mary Then you give us one!
Mark I'm not the Head Foreman.
Piper He's only responsible for his own little team, you see. It's demarcation.
Mary Oh sod demarcation! (*She rounds on Piper*) And what were you doing in our woods?
Piper Relieving myself.
Mary You've seen them, haven't you? You've seen all those rabbits and pheasants!
Piper (*retreating*) No.
Mary Yes you have!
Piper All right, I have!
Mary (*to Mark*) He's told you, hasn't he?
Mark He mentioned it.
Mary (*to Piper*) You've told everybody! We're the people who throw presents away!
Piper I haven't! I haven't!

Brian enters with his tool-bag

Brian Morning all.
Mary
Jim } (*together, rattily*) Good-morning Brian!
Mark
Piper

Act II Scene 3   59

They all look guilty, as if realizing how rude they are being

Brian Sorry I'm late. I had to ——
Jim I'm sorry Brian. How's your wife?
Mary Yes, how is she, Brian?
Brian It was benign.

This is obviously genuine good news for everybody

  I shat bricks waiting. Sorry.
Mary That's all right.
Brian As a matter of fact, she's come home.
Mary Oh I am glad.
Jim That's terrific.
Piper Did you *want* her to come home?

Silence

Brian Anyway, how are things going here?

Behind Jim and Mary's backs, Mark makes "don't ask" signs

  Oh.
Mark We'll get on then, shall we?

  Brian and Mark exit into the extension

Piper (*moving to Mary*) I only told Mark — honest.

  Piper exits into the extension

Jim All those people yesterday. I really thought ——
Mary So did I. So did I.
Jim A "Blitz"!
Mary A one-day "Blitz"!
Jim Where did they all go?
Mary Away from us. We don't rank, do we? We're not seeded. Whatever David's scheme of things is, we come very low on the list.
Jim What did you do in the war, Daddy?
Mary What?

Jim What did you do in the war, Daddy? "I got trampled on by a builder!"
Mary No!
Jim No?
Mary What about a solicitor's letter?
Jim We can't afford to pay a solicitor to pick up a pen, let alone write a letter.
Mary It would have been cheaper to just move house. But no, I had to stay here! "I can help," I said. "I can go back to teaching," I said. Nobody wants supply teachers any more!
Jim We didn't know that then. And look, don't forget. We agreed about the extension.
Mary And you haven't been trampled on!
Jim No? "I must have touched a nerve," that's what I said. Big man! One day's action I produced. One stinking day!
Mary Oh love. (*She looks off* R) Here he comes.
Jim No waffle, right?
Mary No waffle.

They set themselves

David enters cheerfully R, *carrying two boxes*

David Morning Jim, morning Mary! Funny isn't it? I didn't have to go down. He came up. (*He gives the boxes to Jim*) There you are. For you. A present.
Mary What is it?
David Oysters.
Mary Oysters?
Jim Oh. It's very kind of you to remember, David, but we don't need them now.
Mary Why did we need oysters?
Jim We didn't need them. They were just mooted.
Mary Why should oysters be mooted?
David I'm slow! If I put two and two together, you're pregnant, Mary.
Mary Well yes I am, but ...
David Oh my dear girl! May I, Jim? (*He kisses Mary's cheek*) I'm really pleased for you. I'm delighted! (*He shakes hands with Jim*). And many congratulations to you, Jim, many congratulations.
Jim Thank you.
Mary Thank you.
David You're quite well, Mary?
Mary Yes thank you. I'm fine.

Act II Scene 3

David What a lovely time to be born. Just as spring's coming.
Mary Our extension will be finished by then, will it?
David God bless your heart, of course it will be. We're coming into the home straight now.
Mary We wanted to talk to you about that.
David Yes of course. Is it hot or is it just me?
Mary No, it isn't particularly hot. This finishing straight?
David Rounding the final bend.
Jim Whichever. David, about yesterday ...
David And — and this is a vital link — the new windows will be here Tuesday.
Jim What about yesterday?
David I bet your eyes popped.
Mary They're not popping today.
David We call that a "Blitz" in the trade, you know.
Jim Yes, we know what you call it. Where is everybody today?
David You've got Brian back. I know that because he phoned in. It's grand news about his wife, isn't it?
Mary It's wonderful news.
David Worried sick he must have been.
Jim Yes, he must have been.
David Doesn't like showing it, Brian. He's like that. But he must have been worried sick.
Mary Of course. Anyway ——
David Let alone his good lady herself. With women, you see ——
Mary Yes David, with women. Well I'm a woman and we are talking about the eleven extra people we had here yesterday.
David Ah.
Mary Yes. "Ah."
Jim Where are they, David?
David (*loosening his tie*) It is close, isn't it?
Jim Where are they, David?
David The thing is this, you see, being a builder is not like being a general. Not that I'm having a go at our armed forces because I've got the utmost respect for them — I always have had. But it's not the same thing. Now you take a general ——
Mary Oh God!
David A general — at least a general worth his salt — always maintains a strategic reserve, ready to throw into the line wherever there's a weakness.

But a builder can't. He can't plan like that. A builder has to deploy all of his front-line troops all the time.

Jim I don't see ——

David Hear me out, Jim, and you will. Now what a builder has to do is spot a weakness and then re-deploy as many troops as he can. He has to think on his feet, you see. That's what I did yesterday. "Jim and Mary," I thought. "Plug the gap," I thought. "Throw in some troops because, my goodness me, if they don't deserve it, who does?" I thought. We call it a "Blitz" in the trade, you know.

Mary You said that.

David So I did. I don't want to be a nuisance, Mary, but do you think I could have a glass of water?

Mary Yes, I'll get you one.

Mary exits into the house

David That is wonderful news about the baby, Jim. You must be thrilled.

Jim Yes, we are naturally. This "Blitz" ...?

David Very effective, I bet.

Jim Yes it was, but it was also very short.

David You're taking me to task about that, aren't you?

Jim Yes. Yes I am.

David Well that's your privilege, but I should say this. There are other jobs I could have sent them to, Jim, but I didn't. I gave them to you.

Jim For one day!

David Do you know how many man-hours that is?

Jim Yes. Not enough!

Mary enters from the house with a glass of water

David Now hold on a minute, Jim.

Jim No, you hold on a minute! We're not seeded are we?

Mary That's what I said. Here's your water, David.

David Much obliged. Seeded?

Jim Like Wimbledon. The tennis.

David Oh I can't get along with tennis. I never watch it. Cheers. (*He drinks*) Now cricket — you give me a good game of cricket to watch, and I'm a happy man. If you have a little boy, you teach him how to play cricket — it's character-building.

Act II Scene 3

Mary Why are we talking about cricket?
David It was Jim talking about tennis.
Jim I was not talking about tennis.
David You brought Wimbledon up.
Jim It was a metaphor.
David What for?
Jim Us being mucked about!
David Do you seriously call yesterday being mucked about? They were all working up at The Manor you know, those lads. But as soon as I knew they weren't needed for the day ... Well I'm sorry, but if you call that being mucked about, we have a very different interpretation of the phrase altogether.
Mary We're not complaining about yesterday. We loved yesterday.
Jim (*realizing what David has just said*) What do you mean, they weren't needed at The Manor for the day?
David What I say.
Jim *Why* weren't they needed?
David There's a little boy up there, you see.
Mary He's not ill, is he?
David No Mary, he's not ill. But it was his fifth birthday you see.
Mary That doesn't explain anything.
David If I might be allowed to finish.
Mary Sorry.
David Well, they were going to have a party for him, naturally — a marquee and an entertainer, you know. Well it stands to reason, doesn't it? The parents quite naturally didn't want to spoil his little party by having noisy workmen all over the place. Hence the day.
Jim I'm a teacher.
David Yes, I know.
Jim You get insulted quite a lot, being a teacher. Kids are quite good at insults. But you, David, you have just topped the lot!
David I beg your pardon?
Jim A child's fifth birthday party and you take eleven men away so the noise won't spoil it. What do we have to do to get eleven men in the first place — produce a telegram from the Queen on my hundredth birthday?
David You had them yesterday.
Jim Yes, but not because you thought we'd earned them. Because it was convenient. Better than sending them all home for the day, wasn't it?
David Now see here, Jim ——

Jim And I'll tell you why. We're ordinary, that's why. If I were somebody you *needed* we'd get some action. If I were somebody you imagine to have social status — like Harris the airline pilot — I'd get some action. If I were somebody famous I'd get some action because it would make good publicity for you! Something to boast about. "Oh yes, I do all the pop stars' houses, you know. I'm on first-name terms with all of them!"

David I don't know any pop stars.

Jim Whatever. Or shouters.

David Who?

Jim Shouters! They get action. Shout as a way of life and things happen, don't they? Or chuck money. But we don't have any money to chuck. This isn't some middle-class whim! It's everything we've got! The Manor, you see. I'm sick of hearing about the bloody Manor! I assume if a door knob falls off at The Manor, you have six men round there before it hits the ground!

David (*showing signs of feeling unwell*) I've had to concentrate on The Manor, Jim. They've got a penalty clause. Do you mind if I sit down?

Jim (*too fired up to notice David's state*) Oh that's what it takes now, is it? A penalty clause! What happened to somebody's word? What happened to somebody doing their best just because they promised to?

David (*staggering towards a chair*) I — I —

Mary (*worried*) Jim!

Jim Well I've had it! I've had it with being mucked about from arsehole to breakfast time just because I'm a nobody!

David fails to reach the chair and collapses. Mary goes over to David and kneels beside him

Mary Oh Jim!

Jim What's the matter with him?

Mary I think he's having a heart attack!

Jim Oh my God, Mary, I've killed him!

CURTAIN

Scene 4

Three months later

So far as we can see, the extension is finished. The scaffolding and most of the debris from the lawn have gone

Brian is sweeping up the patio and smoking a cigarette

Piper comes on R, pushing a wheelbarrow

Piper (*over his shoulder*) No, that's right Ernie. You stay on the lorry. Don't help anybody carry anything will you? Don't put yourself out!
Brian Have you two had a lovers' tiff?
Piper Well look at him! "I'll help load when things arrive at my lorry," he says. He doesn't function off that lorry of his.
Brian I thought you were a great advocate of demarcation?
Piper Not when I'm not doing it! (*He starts to load the wheelbarrow with debris*)

Brian helps Piper

Piper What are you doing?
Brian I'm helping.
Piper You're a carpenter.
Brian So was Jesus.
Piper What's Jesus got to do with it?
Brian It was a small Biblical joke.
Piper Why?
Brian Now that is a large Biblical question.
Piper Are you going funny?
Brian No. I just want to get home.
Piper Oh yes? You still playing at being married again, are you?
Brian Something like that, yes.
Piper I'm off the idea of marriage altogether.
Brian I don't blame you. It's a silly idea when you're still in short trousers, isn't it? Well go on! I'm not wheeling your barrow for you as well.

Piper starts to wheel the barrow towards the exit R

Hey Piper! Come here! Come here!

Piper backs the barrow to Brian, who drops his cigarette end into it

Off you go.

Piper says the following as he wheels the barrow off towards the gate R

Piper I'm sorry to disturb you, Ernie your Eminence! I've got another barrow-load for you.

He exits

Brian sweeps his pile of dirt and sand under the patio seat

Mary comes out of the house. She is three months pregnant. She looks around her in half-wonderment

Brian You're not hallucinating. We really are going.
Mary It's funny. I don't even know how I feel.
Brian You've done well.
Mary No.
Brian You'd be surprised.
Mary Jim should be back from the hospital soon.

Mary exits into the house

Brian heads for the exit R

Piper enters R *with the wheelbarrow, meeting Brian*

Piper That was the sum total of your assistance, was it?
Brian I don't want the world to find out how nice I really am.

He exits

Piper I don't think there's much chance of the world finding out!

Piper starts to load more debris into the barrow

Act II Scene 4

Mark enters R. *He wears a dark suit and a black tie*

Piper How did it go then?
Mark Why do people always ask how funerals go? They're funerals aren't they? There's only one way they can go. Like funerals.
Piper You had a good time then.
Mark I thought you'd have cleared this lot up by now.
Piper Now there speaks the new Head Foreman.
Mark Jealous?
Piper Let down.
Mark Why?
Piper Well, it's you selling your soul, really, isn't it? I was under the impression that you were going out on your own to set the building trade to rights. I don't know what made me think that. You talking about it about fifty times a week I suppose.
Mark I have not sold my soul.
Piper You got a raise.
Mark I have not sold my soul! I still believe in things.
Piper Oh yes. Like I believe in fairies.
Mark Well come on. We've got to start on the Vicar's damp course tomorrow.
Piper Yes Guv'nor. Right Guv'nor!

Mark and Piper start to load the barrow

Piper When did you tell the Vicar we'd be starting?
Mark Last Wednesday.
Piper That's a good start isn't it — lying to a man of the cloth?

Brian enters R *with his tool-bag*

Brian Now that's some sort of record. I'm actually leaving with all the tools I arrived with. (*He takes a chisel from Piper's back pocket and then holds out his hand*)

Piper takes a tape measure from his pocket and hands it over

Brian How did the funeral go then?
Mark It was excruciatingly funny!
Piper Take no notice. He's power-crazed.

Jim enters. He is very much quieter than when we last saw him. He carries a packet of grass seed

Jim Hallo lads.
Mark ⎫
Piper ⎬ (*together, quietly*) Hallo Mr Baxter.
Brian ⎭
Jim How did the funeral go, Mark?
Mark Oh very nice. Very tasteful.
Jim Oh good. Did you play cricket at the weekend?
Mark It's the football season.
Jim So it is. So it is.
Piper They lost twenty-eight — nil.
Jim I bought some grass seed.

They all nod

Brian I chamfered the gatepost by the way.
Jim Oh good.
Piper (*referring to the wheelbarrow*) Of course, I *can* run this up the boards by myself.
Mark Come on!

Mark and Piper exit R with the wheelbarrow

Brian Well, I'll say "Cheerio" then.
Jim Right. (*Calling*) Mary! Brian's going!
Brian You'll be back at school soon then?
Jim Two weeks, yes. They've been very good about the sick-leave. Very good.

Mary enters from the house carrying three envelopes. She hands one to Brian

Mary It isn't much, Brian, but thank you.
Brian Oh now you shouldn't have done that!(*He opens the envelope to find that it really isn't much*) Thank you. You've got a nice house here you know.
Mary I'm glad things worked out for you and your wife.
Brian Yes they have — more or less.
Mary More or less?

Act II Scene 4

Brian You'll laugh at this. It's not exactly a condition on her coming back for good. Not exactly a condition — but it is getting mentioned a lot.
Mary What is?
Brian She wants an extension on our house. I said you'd laugh.
Jim We'll think of you.
Brian I bet you will. Cheerio then.
Jim Bye Brian.

Mary kisses Brian's cheek

Mary Bye Brian.

Brian heads for the exit R

Mark and Piper enter R and meet Brian

Piper See you at the Vicarage.
Brian I don't know where you're going to pee. There's no garden to speak of at all there.

Brian exits R

There is the sound of a lorry starting up

Mark (*looking off* R) Mind the gatepost Ernie!
Piper (*looking off* R) You're too close, you nerk!
Brian (*off*) I've just chamfered that!

Jim, Mary, Mark and Piper brace themselves for the sound of a crash but it never comes

Mark (*holding up his thumb and forefinger*) By that much.
Jim A sort of last-minute thrill.
Mark Well then.
Jim Well then.

There is a sense of half-embarrassed anti-climax

Mary (*holding out the other two envelopes to Mark and Piper*) We'd like you to take this. It isn't much, but——

Piper extends his hand

Mark (*knocking Piper's hand down*) No. We've talked about this, and we've — decided we can't.

This is obviously news to Piper

You haven't had the easiest time, but you've never taken it out on us, which some do, so we'd like you to buy something for the baby instead, wouldn't we, Piper?
Piper (*without enthusiasm*) Yes.

Mary begins to cry

(*Sticking out his hand again*) Look, if it's going to upset you ——

Mark slaps Piper's hand down again

Mary It's kindness. It's ridiculous. Kindness makes me cry now. Sorry.
Jim Well thanks very much, lads. We'll buy him a little trowel or something. And look, if you're ever passing ...
Mark Oh yes, of course. Cheerio then.
Mary (*kissing Mark's cheek*) Goodbye Mark.
Jim Bye Mark.
Mark Good luck with the ——
Jim Thanks. Bye Piper.
Mary Bye Piper. (*She moves to kiss Piper's cheek*)
Piper (*ducking away*) Cheers.

Mark and Piper exit R

Mary I feel an absolute fool.
Jim They're good lads.
Mary I'll almost miss them.
Jim Only "almost" though.
Mary Yes. Only "almost".

They cuddle

It's finished. It's actually finished.
Jim We ought to do something. We ought to celebrate.
Mary Let's just sit and listen to the silence.

Act II Scene 4

They sit on the patio seat

Jim I bought some grass seed.
Mary Isn't the builder supposed to make good the lawn?
Jim We don't want to know about that, do we?
Mary No. Quite right.
Jim I can go back to school in two weeks' time.
Mary You shouldn't have blamed yourself you know.
Jim That's what the therapist kept saying.
Mary You do believe her?
Jim I suppose so. Either way, I'm going back to being a pebble.
Mary What?
Jim A pebble. I tried to be a rock, you see. It didn't come off, did it?
Mary Brian said we did well.
Jim Did he? Well, we stopped short of attempting suicide, so I suppose we must have done. We had almost everything else though, didn't we? Rows, tears, lies, betrayals. We had all the makings of a half-way decent Greek tragedy.
Mary They didn't have tranquillizers in Greek tragedies.
Jim Or therapists.
Mary I wonder how Brian will stand up to *his* extension?
Jim Well if it's anything like a doctor having to go into hospital ...
Mary (*looking off* R) Well, look who's here.

David enters R. He is walking with a stick and is somewhat quieter in his manner than before

David Good news! The lads will definitely finish clearing up by ... Oh, they already have.
Mary How are you, David? Come and sit down.
Jim Yes, how are you, David? How are you feeling?
David Oh well you know, I'm getting about more. (*He sits*) Of course, the funeral pulled me down a bit. It went marvellously well though. Gwen was a tower of course.
Jim Gwen?
David Old Ronnie's daughter — a wonderful woman despite her neck. Oh Mary, "Thank you very much for the flowers," she said.
Mary They weren't much.
David They were appreciated, that's the thing. Poor old Ronnie. It doesn't seem yesterday that I was saying he'd go on for ever. Still, none of us do and nobody knows that better than someone who's had a warning.

Jim The er ——?

David (*beginning to enjoy a bit of self-pity*) Yes. "A warning." That's what the hospital said. Funny feeling, getting a warning. It's like facing the rest of your life with the lights stuck on amber.

Jim and Mary smile at David's performance

Something I said?

Jim No, no. We're just happy.

David Of course you are, of course you are. I'm sorry these last weeks have dragged on a bit, but not being able to get about as much as I'd like to, you see ... I told you why we got held up by the plasterers, didn't I?

Jim No, I don't think we heard that one.

David Well — and I know this almost defies belief until you hear the whole story — it was the Channel Tunnel, you see. Not that the plasterers were on the Channel Tunnel, but Harry's nephew who was ——

Mary David, it doesn't matter. They came in the end. Everybody came in the end. And now everybody's gone and it's all over.

David I'm proud of this job, you know, proud of the workmanship. It's properly done.

Jim Much admired.

David It's properly priced too. I've never claimed to be the cheapest around, but there's not a nail or a screw unaccounted for.

Jim That's the funny thing.

David Funny?

Jim Yes. The workmanship and the price. They're the two things we never questioned for a minute.

David I take that as a compliment.

Mary We questioned a lot of other things.

David I'm not a cruel man, Mary. I *have* to spread my lads thin, you see. A builder *has* to be over-stretched. I've got thirty-five people depending on me for a living. I don't go around being cruel willy-nilly. Anyway, if this should turn out to be the last job I ever see through to completion, well I'll go out with pride.

Mary Oh, come on, David. You'll go on forever.

David That's what I used to say to old Ronnie Randall. He was decorated, you know.

Jim Was he?

David I suppose that once you've had a — well, let's keep calling it a "warning" — well, do you put your Autumn bulbs in?

Act II Scene 4

Mary I thought we'd cornered the market in self-pity. You're turning it into an art form.
David Beg pardon?
Mary Well really! "Do you put your Autumn bulbs in?" Think of all the extensions you've still got to do. Think of all the anxieties you've got to ease — all the anger and sheer bloody frustration you've got to calm. Think of all the old excuses you can re-cycle. Think of all the new ones you haven't even made up. It's your life-blood, David. Even with Life's traffic lights stuck on amber, it's your life-blood.
David I've had to give up shooting, you know.
Mary You don't need a shotgun. You've already got an extra weapon in your armoury.
David I'm not with you.
Mary "The warning!" Think about it. How can anybody ever shout at you again? How can anyone risk upsetting you again? It's not an extra weapon, it's the ultimate weapon.
David Good heavens above, Mary, you don't seriously think I'd use my health?
Mary Why not? You've used everyone else's.
David Jim?
Jim It has a ring to it, doesn't it? "Press me on why the carpenter's three weeks late and I'll keel over in front of you!"
David (*deciding that the best thing to do is take Jim's remark as a joke*) That's something I've always liked about you two — your sense of humour. You do it with such straight faces too, that's the trick.

Mary and Jim are happy enough not to argue

(*Getting up*) Well, I'd better get round to the Vicarage. His damp course has gone and I promised we'd start last Tuesday. About the lawn ...
Jim We'll do the lawn.
David Oh. Well, "He who hesitates ..." and so on.
Jim Bye bye, David.
David (*shaking Jim's hand*) I'm sorry about the therapy.
Jim I think of that as my "warning."
David Bye Mary.

Mary kisses David's cheek

Mary Don't get obsessive about the traffic lights.
David No. And if I ever do go shooting again ...

Mary Well ——

Jim You know us, David. You shoot it, we'll throw it down the garden.

David obviously isn't sure whether to take this as a joke

David Bye then!

David exits R, forgetting his stick; Jim and Mary don't notice either

Mary God help the Vicar.
Jim Well he is on the staff, so to speak.
Mary Let's start lunch. Jim?
Jim (*a little pre-occupied*) Um?
Mary Are you all right?
Jim Yes, I'm all right. I did David an injustice you know.
Mary You did David ——? When?
Jim After I stopped feeling guilty. It didn't last long — just a couple of days I suppose — but I couldn't get the thought out of my mind. More of a suspicion really. I couldn't stop wondering whether it was all a trick. Like your ultimate weapon. But not a weapon — a trick.
Mary David's heart attack?
Jim Yes. It sounds ridiculous now.
Mary Well of course it does. Even David couldn't fake a thing like that. I mean, we phoned for an ambulance.
Jim I know. I know.
Mary And an ambulance came — a real ambulance.
Jim I know. I just had this mad thought that Ernie was driving it, wearing a false moustache.
Mary David was taken to hospital. Who was the doctor who looked after him — Brian with his chisel?
Jim I said it was ridiculous.
Mary It was. I know David has pulled some strokes, but stage-managing a heart attack ... Even David ...
Jim Well, of course that's what I told myself in the end. Even David ...

But a tiny seed of doubt, however absurd, has been planted. They try to shake the thought

Jim
Mary } (*together*) No. No!

Act II Scene 4

They exit into the house and close the door

David enters R to reclaim his stick. He walks quite normally. He picks up the stick, then glances at the house, perhaps remembering Mary's words

He walks off R, leaning heavily on the stick

CURTAIN

FURNITURE AND PROPERTY LIST

ACT 1

Scene 1

On stage: Scaffolding
Ladders
Garden seat
Two garden chairs
Bench
Timber
Bricks
Hand-built truss
Paving slabs
Cement mixer
Tray. *On it*: two mugs of tea
Sandwiches for **Mark** and **Piper**

Off stage: Briefcase (**Jim**)

Personal: **David**: notebook, pen, watch (all used throughout)

Scene 2

Set: Pile of cement

Off stage: Brace of pheasants (**David**)
Saw horse, tool-bag. *In it*: tenon saw, loaf of bread, tub of butter, chisel (**Brian**)
Tin of biscuits (**Jim**)
Tray. *On it*: coffee mugs, jug of milk, jar of Coffee-Mate (**Mary**)
Shopping bag (**Mary**)

Personal: **Mark**: packet of mints
Brian: slice of ham (in jacket pocket)

ACT II

Scene 1

Strike: Truss

Set: Slates
Sink unit
Other bathroom fittings

Off stage: Toilet (**Mark**)
Bidet (**Piper**)
Tray. *On it*: mugs, milk, sugar, biscuits (**Jim**)
Teapot (**Mary**)
Pieces of chalk (**Piper**)
Portable telephone (**Jim**)
Bath (**Mark** and **Piper**)
Cup (**Mary**)

Personal: Brian: car keys

Scene 2

Off stage: Shopping (**Mary**)
Teddy bear (**Jim**)
Plumbing equipment (**Piper**)
A can each of lager and soft drink (**Mary**)

Scene 3

Off stage: Overnight bags (**Jim** and **Mary**)
Tool-bag (**Brian**)
Two boxes (**David**)

Scene 4

Strike: Scaffolding
Ladders
Most of the debris from the lawn

Set: Broom for **Brian**

Off stage: Wheelbarrow (**Piper**)
Tool-bag (**Brian**)
Grass seed (**Jim**)
Three envelopes (**Mary**)
Stick (**David**)

Personal: **Brian**: cigarette
Piper: chisel, tape measure

LIGHTING PLOT

Practical fittings required: nil

Exterior. A garden

ACT I SCENE 1

To open: General exterior lighting

No cues

ACT I SCENE 2

To open: General exterior lighting

No cues

ACT II SCENE 1

To open: General exterior lighting

No cues

ACT II SCENE 2

To open: General exterior lighting

No cues

ACT II SCENE 3

To open: General exterior lighting

No cues

ACT II SCENE 4

To open: General exterior lighting

No cues

EFFECTS PLOT

ACT I

Cue 1	**Piper:** "... nail it to his forehead." *Lorry in low gear; horn sounds*	(Page 3)
Cue 2	**Piper:** "Ernie!" *Thump and rending of wood*	(Page 3)
Cue 3	**Mary:** "Yes." *Car pulls up*	(Page 5)
Cue 4	**Jim:** "Oh, dear. Bad luck, that." *Car approaches and continues past*	(Page 11)
Cue 5	**David** enters *High-pitched whine of an angle-ginder*	(Page 14)
Cue 6	**David:** "I want you and Piper to ——" *Angle-grinder noise stops*	(Page 14)
Cue 7	**Piper** exits L *Angle-grinder noise starts again; stops during following dialogue*	(Page 15)
Cue 8	**David** heads for the exit R *Sawing*	(Page 29)
Cue 9	**David:** "Brian?" *Sawing stops*	(Page 29)

ACT II

Cue 10	As Scene 1 opens *Hammering and sawing*	(Page 38)
Cue 11	**Mark, Piper** and **Brian** hide the slates *Telephone rings*	(Page 47)

Cue 12	**David** exits; **Jim** sits down *Telephone rings*	(Page 50)
Cue 13	As SCENE 2 opens *Hammering, sawing, drilling etc.*	(Page 51)
Cue 14	As SCENE 3 opens *Car approaches and pulls up*	(Page 56)
Cue 15	**Brian** exits R *Lorry starts up*	(Page 69)

PRINTED IN GREAT BRITAIN BY
THE LONGDUNN PRESS LTD., BRISTOL.

www.ingramcontent.com/pod-product-compliance
Ingram Content Group UK Ltd.
Pitfield, Milton Keynes, MK11 3LW, UK
UKHW021844210426
5322IPUK00022B/466